Asian Collection

HANDBOOK

Chinese, Tang dynasty, 7th century

Pair of guardian figures
Earthenware with traces of pigment over white slip;
heights 93 and 92 cm

Purchased by the Art Gallery of New South Wales Foundation 1990

Asian Collection
HANDBOOK

Jacqueline Menzies

with an introduction
by Edmund Capon

ART GALLERY OF NEW SOUTH WALES

This Handbook has been produced with funds provided
by the Art Gallery Society of New South Wales

Among many others, the Gallery wishes to acknowledge the
support of the following for the Asian art collections:

Eugene Anchugov
Art Gallery Society of New South Wales
Fred and Ella Bodor and family
Sydney Cooper
Graham E. Fraser
Laurence G. Harrison
Idemitsu Kosan Co. Ltd
Rev. Muneharu Kurozumi
Dr Weiping Liu
Kenneth and Yasuko Myer
The Sidney Myer Fund
J. Hepburn Myrtle
Klaus Naumann
Mrs Orwell Phillips and family
Randall Reed
Norman Sparnon
Ed and Goldie Sternberg
Freddy Storch

Produced for the Art Gallery of New South Wales
by The Beagle Press, Sydney
Designed by Wing Ping Tong
Text by Jacqueline Menzies, Curator of Asian Art
Photography by Ray Woodbury and Timothy Marshall
Colour separations by Quadrascan Graphics
Printed by Frank Daniels Pty Ltd, Perth

Published 1990 by the Trustees,
Art Gallery of New South Wales,
Art Gallery Road, Sydney, Australia 2000
Telephone (02) 225 1700

ISBN 0 7305 7455 5

COVER
KATSUKAWA SHUN'EI, Japanese, 1762-1819
Portrait of a beautiful woman (*bijin*)
Hanging scroll; ink and colours on silk, 84 × 33 cm
Purchased 1985

BACK COVER
Calligraphy by Ota Nampo (1749-1823)
written on the painting by Shun'ei

CONTENTS

FOREWORD   7

INTRODUCTION   9

EARLY CHINESE ART   18

CHINESE PORCELAIN   30

CHINESE PAINTING   42

JAPANESE PAINTING   53

JAPANESE ART   70

SOUTH-EAST ASIAN ART   83

CHRONOLOGICAL TABLES   96

DETAIL
UNKOKU TŌEKI, Japanese, 1591–1644

Landscape
Pair of six-fold screens; ink, slight colour and
gold wash on paper, each screen 154.5 × 353 cm

Purchased with funds donated by Kenneth Myer 1986

FOREWORD

The beginnings of the Asian collections of the Gallery date back to the gift in 1879 by the Japanese Government, of a large group of Japanese ceramics and bronzes that had been shown in the International Exhibition that same year. It was not however until 1979, exactly 100 years later, that the Asian Department was formally established. Since that time our collections have developed strongly with a special emphasis upon the arts of Japan.

A notable event was the gift in 1962 by Sydney Cooper of a group of Chinese pottery tomb figures and other ceramics, followed by the determined efforts of Mr Hepburn Myrtle to add fine examples of Ming and Qing porcelain. Ceramics, therefore, predominate in the Chinese collection but recent acquisitions of 20th century Chinese paintings and early Buddhist sculpture have added breadth to more properly represent the arts of China.

The Japanese collections, with the extraordinarily generous support of Mr Kenneth Myer, have developed strongly in recent years. Whilst screens and paintings have been the particular focus of our efforts it is the Gallery's policy to represent the arts of Japan in as comprehensive a manner as possible.

The Asian collections of the Gallery have developed significantly in the last decade and that growth has only been possible through the generous support of a number of individuals whose concern for the Gallery and for Asian art has expressed itself in the most tangible way, through gifts of works of art and in the provision of funds for acquisitions. In particular the Gallery acknowledges the support of Mr Kenneth Myer, Mr and Mrs Ed Sternberg, Mr Hepburn Myrtle and Mr Freddy Storch who, among others, have ensured and continue to ensure the future of our Asian art collections.

The opening of the Asian Gallery, incorporating the Japan Gallery, for which we express our gratitude to the Idemitsu Kosan Co. Ltd and the Japan Foundation for their considerable financial support, and the Sternberg Gallery of Chinese Art, is a notable milestone in the history of the Gallery. It is the final stage of the major new extensions of the Gallery that were opened in December 1988 and the initial publication of this Handbook, so generously funded by the Art Gallery Society of New South Wales, coincides with that event.

EDMUND CAPON DIRECTOR

WANG ZHEN, Chinese, 1867–1938

Nine years facing the wall

Hanging scroll; ink and colours on paper, 148.3 × 80.5 cm

Purchased 1989

INTRODUCTION

BY EDMUND CAPON

The geography of East Asia ranges from tropical jungles to frozen peaks, from lush temperate pastures to arid deserts; the cultures, languages and ideologies of the region are as varied and yet there lurk beneath the surface of all those rich qualities and attitudes some common grounds. From a Western perspective it is all too easy to view East Asia as one culture and whilst there is some validity to such a view in the broadest sense, the local variations that have evolved and emerged over centuries of accepting, absorbing and sometimes defraying influences, invasions and ideas, have created a family of cultures, related but distinctive. The purpose of this Handbook is to introduce the material culture, the arts, of those East Asian cultures as represented in the collections of this Gallery. We cannot pretend that our representation of the arts of China, Japan, Korea and Southeast Asia is complete but it is sufficient in quantity and quality to provide an evocative picture of the riches and the distinctions of those arts.

There can be no disputing the fact that China is the cultural arbiter of the region. The arts of the whole of East Asia have been constantly and powerfully influenced by the art of civilization's longest still surviving identifiable culture; the arts and attitudes of China today are the natural inheritors in a culture that may be traced directly back through history to China's neolithic age of the 5th to 3rd millennium BC. Having evolved and grown into such a powerful identity, virtually unhindered and largely uninfluenced by other civilizations, the culture of China has become as impregnable as any in the history of civilization. With such strength and identity it became the ultimate source of inspiration for those emerging cultures on her periphery.

Amongst the most potent of those influences emanating from China was that determined by the means of communication, that is writing, and China's distinctive form, based originally on graphic pictographs that evolved into a most eloquent form of writing and self-expression, lies at the roots of the Japanese language. Whilst Korean belongs to the Ural-Altaic family of languages it too contains a large proportion of Chinese influence and at times in her history, such as the Unified Silla period (AD668–935) Chinese was the written language of the court, official and scholarly worlds. And if we look at other of China's more distinctive artistic achievements, such as painting which is after all directly related to the art of writing

Korean, Koryo period (918–1392)
Cupstand of lotus form
Celadon; 6 × 14.5 cm
Gift of J. Hepburn Myrtle 1989

or calligraphy, and ceramics, we again find the influences of the Chinese artists and craftsmen surfacing throughout East Asia. However it must be recognised that influences are but inspirations and the arts created within the Chinese sphere of influence were not slavish copies, for each country achieved national identity in its artistic endeavour; the tea bowls of Japan inspired originally by the wares of Song China and the rustic wares of Korea are unmistakably Japanese; Korean celadons are related to their Chinese counterparts but retain a distinctive Korean flavour in their detail and decoration; so too the blue and white wares of Vietnam, the ink paintings and the elegant lacquers of Japan. All have their links with China, all express an aesthetic that is indisputably Chinese and East Asian, but all retain a distinction and sense of individuality determined by local characteristics and attitudes.

There was, however, another tenacious link across East Asia that was not born of China,— the faith of Buddhism. As Buddhism spread from India, across the wastes of Central Asia into China in the 1st and 2nd centuries AD and thence to Korea and Japan, it brought with it an iconography and an art that has continued to inspire the creative instincts down to the present day and also provide another persuasive cultural umbrella for the region. Indeed from the 4th to the 10th centuries Buddhism united the region in an unprecedented manner that underwrote ideological, attitudinal and artistic patterns which contributed significantly to that sense of overall cultural unity. Whilst, from the 14th century Buddhism in

Gandharan, c. 3rd century AD
Figure of Buddha
Grey schist; height 109 cm
Gift of Josef and Regina Neumann
1986

Chinese, Eastern Wei dynasty
(534–550 AD)

Standing Sakyamuni Buddha flanked
by two Bodhisattvas
Carved limestone stele; height 61 cm

Purchased 1988

its homeland, India, was virtually consumed under the onslaught of Islam, the faith continued to flourish in East Asia. Probably the most important reason for its success was its essentially contemplative nature that found a sympathetic audience among the peoples of East Asia who were always attracted towards their traditional mystic and meditative philosophies based on a veneration for the natural world.

Chinese, Song dynasty
12th–13th century

Figure of Guanyin
Carved and painted wood;
height 114 cm

Bequest of Sydney Cooper 1982

The art of Buddhism is, therefore, a fitting starting point for any introduction to the arts of East Asia and one area in which this Gallery has sought selected works. The function of art in the service of Buddhism was largely iconographical and to a lesser extent to provide the paraphernalia of ritual. As an iconographical art it

Japanese, 12th century

Seated image of Amida Buddha
Nutmeg wood; height 53 cm
(with base 96.5 cm)

Purchased with assistance from the
W. H. Nolan Bequest Fund 1984

was basically figurative and confined to the arts of painting and
sculpture but in so far as East Asia was concerned the significant
contribution of Buddhism was to introduce a new aesthetic and a
new dimension to her arts. For example, monumental figurative
sculpture was a virtually alien tradition to the art of China until the

advent of Buddhism which continued to provide the motive for the art from its inception in China around the 3rd/4th century to the end of dynastic China at the beginning of the 20th century.

The origins of the sculptural style of Buddhist art in China, and thus eventually in Korea and Japan, lie not in India but in the Gandharan art of Pakistan. The very earliest surviving Buddhist sculptures in China, dating to the early 4th century, clearly show that dependence upon the Gandharan style with their close-fitting robes enveloping a figure of sound proportions and just a hint of sensuality. This was a style that was to reach its zenith in the second half of the 5th century in the massive rock-hewn carvings of Buddha images at the Yungang cave temples near Datong in northern Shanxi province. By the early 6th century a dramatic change in approach had taken place and Chinese Buddhist sculpture adopted a style and aesthetic that, in its formalism and stylish austerity, more accurately reflected Chinese traditions and which is well illustrated in the Gallery's beautiful small limestone stele datable to the Eastern Wei dynasty (AD534–550). By the end of the 6th century fresh influences, this time ultimately from India, received through China's contacts along the Silk Routes, revived a sense of naturalism in Buddhist sculpture which imbued the art during the Tang dynasty (AD618–906) with a grace and fluency that is illustrated in the Gallery's late 7th/early 8th century carved limestone torso of a Bodhisattva. During the later Tang and succeeding dynasties Buddhism in China became part of the established folklore of the country as opposed to a stern ideological philosophy and its art lost that quality of austere spirituality which had been so characteristic of, for example, the sculptural style of the Wei dynasties in the 6th century and the early Tang dynasty. This more pliant attitude infused the arts of Buddhism with an approachable homely character that is perfectly displayed in a 12th century Song dynasty carved wood figure of the Bodhisattva Guanyin, the traditional Goddess of Mercy.

During the 5th and 6th centuries Japan was much preoccupied with Korea and there was very little direct contact with China. Nevertheless it was at this time that much of Chinese civilization, including Buddhism, travelled to Japan through the Korean peninsula. The advent of Buddhism in Japan probably gave a strong emotional stimulus to the pursuit of things Chinese and learning, including the Chinese writing system, among the courts of Japan with the result that by the end of the 6th century Buddhism had a firm and permanent footing permitting the faith to quietly grow and complement, rather than supplant, the native Shinto religion. Certainly by the 12th century when the Gallery's sublime and serene wood sculpture of Amida Buddha, the Buddha of the Western

Paradise, was carved, Buddhism was confidently part of the Japanese way of life with a background of centuries of evolution and an establishment of many sects and temples, particularly in the Kyoto/Nara region, that still stand and operate to this day.

Whilst in China, from the end of the Tang dynasty onwards, Buddhism has merely survived with few new initiatives or directions other perhaps than Tibetan Lamaism, in Japan the faith flourished inspired by the vitality, individuality and sometimes eccentricity of numerous and often divergent sects. Of these by far the most famous was Zen, which again originated in the gregarious material, intellectual and spiritual atmosphere of Tang dynasty China following the arrival of the monk Bodhidharma at the end of the 6th century. He was devoted to the practice of *dhyana* (or *chan* in Chinese), the discipline of absolute concentration aimed at tranquillizing the mind so that the definition between the finite and the infinite no longer exists. A particular attraction of the Zen sect, apart from its eccentric and often amusing tenets and standards, was a recognition that the Buddha-nature exists in us all and is available to all mankind through the attainment of enlightenment, *wu* in China and *satori* in Japan. Through such enlightenment, that complete union with *sunyata* (the only true reality — that is infinity or the concept of the void), differences do not exist and there is a single fundamental unity of all things. Zen is the absolute quality of absolute infinity — it is the spirit of all things and the spirit of nothing. The appeal of such a philosophy is obvious, and the ideals it proclaims have transcended the centuries. Equally important is that Zen inspired an artistic tradition, particularly in painting and calligraphy, that is as unique and tenacious as the sect itself. The Zen ideal sees purity and reality in spontaneity and nowhere is this better expressed than in the swift and expressive black ink strokes of Zen calligraphy and paintings depicting anything from an enigmatic turnip to a mischievous looking deity. But the concept of Zen and its values was felt beyond its own art for it influenced the whole tradition of *suiboku* ink painting, represented in the Gallery by such artists as Unkoku Tōeki (1591–1644), Kusumi Morikage (c1620–1690) and Nagasawa Rosetsu's odd and humorous depiction of the Zen identities Kanzan and Jittoku.

The great strength of Buddhism is its adaptability. From a single ultimate source the faith has provided a wellspring of ideas, values and opportunities that allowed it to spread throughout East Asia, be adapted and absorbed into the hearts and minds of differing peoples, and above all through its capacity for perpetual interpretation and reinterpretation, to survive. It is indeed a virtual symbol of East Asian cultural and artistic ideals.

NAGASAWA ROSETSU, Japanese
1754–1799
Kanzan and Jittoku
Hanging scroll; ink on paper
157.7 × 81.8 cm
Purchased 1985

EARLY CHINESE ART

Much of our knowledge of ancient China stems from the archaeological excavation of tombs which, in accordance with traditional
Chinese beliefs concerning the afterlife, were stacked with
treasures and paraphernalia reflecting the material and spiritual
concerns of deceased royalty and aristocracy. Before China
evolved into its dynastic history the country was peopled by neolithic age, village-based communities whose cultures are identified
by their ceramic wares. The earliest examples of Chinese art in the
Gallery collections represent this neolithic age which archaeologists
have now determined dates back to the 6th–5th millennium BC.
In the Yellow River valley, generally recognised as the cradle of
Chinese civilization, two principal neolithic cultures have been
identified: the Yangshao centred in Henan province, and the
Longshan culture which originated in north-easterly Shandong province. A later and more westerly branch of the Yangshao culture,
known as the Panshan culture and based in Gansu province, is
represented by typically unglazed, burnished earthenware funerary

Chinese, c. 3rd century BC
Food storage jar (pou)
Stoneware; 21.2 × 33 cm
Gift of the Art Gallery Society 1962

urns decorated with geometric and linear patterns, symbolic in spirit and thus suggestive of ritual or funerary use. At this time and in the succeeding Bronze Age, purely utilitarian ceramics tended to be undecorated apart from occasional patterns achieved from cloth impressions or incisions into the damp clay.

Even as early as the pre-Bronze Age neolithic period the Chinese people have used jade, or more accurately nephrite, for ritual and symbolic purposes. Venerated for its hardness, purity of colour and supposed magic qualities, jade has throughout the history of China played an important role in burial procedures in which various pieces carved into symbolic shapes were placed around the body and miniature carvings of, for example, animals, used to plug the orifices. The most popular ceremonial jade in ancient China was the *bi* disc which, as a symbol of heaven, was usually placed at the head of the deceased. Other such ancient jades included in the collections are the *zong*, a tubular shaped object with a squared section that is traditionally regarded as a symbol of the earth, and the *gui*, a trapezoidal blade, its shape reminiscent of a neolithic stone harvesting knife even down to the perforations along the unsharpened edge.

Bronze ritual vessels of extraordinary technical accomplishment and artistic vision are the hallmark products of China's Bronze Age civilization embracing the Shang (c1600–1027BC) and the Zhou (1027–221BC) dynasties. These elaborate and imaginatively ornamented vessels, together with bronze weapons for both ceremonial and practical use and other accessories such as harness and chariot fittings, cast by means of a ceramic piece-mould and later, in the Zhou dynasty, by the lost-wax or *cire-perdu* technique, are represented in the displays by selected examples. The Shang dynasty also witnessed the creation of China's written language and many bronzes, particularly vessels dating from the succeeding Zhou dynasty, bear inscriptions describing, for example, the circumstances of the dedication of the vessel and the associated ceremony, thereby providing unique information concerning China's ancient history.

The Shang funerary practice of human sacrifice in association with burial was, from the mid-Zhou era, gradually replaced by the more humane tradition of furnishing the tomb with facsimiles; originally wood and later pottery models of humans and animals that had been in the service of the deceased on earth. The Gallery collection includes fine examples of such tomb furniture (*mingqi*) of the Han (206BC–AD220) and Tang (AD618–906) dynasties, which because of their deliberate realism tell us much of the social and political customs such as fashion, hierarchy, agriculture, amusements and architecture of ancient China. Amongst the finest of the

Han dynasty figures in the collection is the standing lady whose distinguished but humble demeanour, with her hands politely clasped within the voluminous sleeves of her costume, suggests that she represents a courtly attendant. It is a figure of extraordinary grace and eloquent simplicity that is characteristic of the sophisticated Han style. Typically for such models the figure was made from moulds, the parts then luted together and the details finished by hand before the firing process. The figure was then covered with a white slip which served as a base for the detail painting of which only traces remain. In the Han dynasty single glaze colours were also used for ornamenting certain, usually animal or architectural, tomb models, but in the Tang dynasty the use of colour and multi-colour glazes was widespread.

Bronzes, including vessels, fittings and accessories, were also found in Han dynasty tombs though generally they were modest in scale and more restrained in form and decoration than those of the preceding Shang and Zhou eras. Of special interest are the mirrors which first appeared in the repertoire of ancient Chinese bronzes in the late Shang and, as the finds in tombs would suggest, became popular in the Han dynasty. The reverse or non-reflective side of the mirror became the vehicle for the expression of all kinds of symbolical and mythological notions. Because they reflected light, they were symbols of light in the eternal darkness of the tomb; because they could expose evil spirits (which can take human form but which have no reflection) they served a protective role. Bronze, however, was expensive and towards the end of the Zhou dynasty, when the metal was in widespread demand for both ritual and practical military purposes, pottery versions of the vessels used in ceremony and burial were introduced. This tradition too is seen in the Asian Gallery with low-fired lead glazed earthenwares very much in the tomb figure tradition and higher-fired stoneware vessels with feldspathic glazes that are often exact replicas in both form and decoration of the classic bronzes of the later Zhou period.

Exhibited with the arts of the Han dynasty are rubbings taken from the carved stone interior walls of the shrines for ancestral offerings that were constructed, in the mid-2nd century of the Eastern Han dynasty, at the site of the burial of the Wu family in Shandong province. Inscriptions in and around the tomb site mention four generations of the Wu family, many of whom were distinguished officials in the bureaucracy of later Han China. The themes of the stories related in the reliefs concern not only traditional mythology such as images of the great mythical emperors of far distant China, the Queen Mother of the West and King of the East, but references to Confucian ideals of female virtue and

Chinese, Han dynasty
(206BC–AD220)
Standing figure
Earthenware with traces of pigment
over white slip; height 40.3 cm
Gift of Sydney Cooper 1962

filial piety and illustrations of real or supposed historical incident. As such they provide a vivid picture of the Han pictorial style, the concerns of the ruling classes and a wonderful parallel to the actual tomb figures.

Following the fall of the Han dynasty, China was embroiled in almost four centuries of internecine conflict and intermittent foreign invasions. And yet this, the so-called period of division when the north fell predominantly under non-Chinese rule and the south remained under Chinese rule, was a surprisingly lively time for the arts with the added inspiration of Buddhism and new contacts with foreign influences, all of which laid the foundations for a flowering of the arts in the Tang dynasty (618–906). There can be no more evocative symbol of this often referred to 'Golden Age' in China's history than the Tang horse, represented in the collections by a number of examples of which the most splendid is the three-colour (*sancai*) glazed model of a horse and rider from a retinue of military figures once placed in the tomb of a member of the royal house, a dignitary or military official. The colourful and imaginative spirit of Tang China, that was so stimulated and enriched by the trade with Western Asia carried on along the ancient Silk Routes, is echoed in the silks, silver work and ceramics of the age. This trade is symbolised in the pottery models of its bearers, the camel, such as the example included in the Gallery displays.

The most elegant of the Tang tomb figures on display are undoubtedly the pair of slender and graceful models of court ladies, often identified as princesses, but possibly dancers whose elaborate costumes and high coiffures were the height of fashion in Tang China. It has been suggested that these figures are dressed to perform the dance to the songs of the Rainbow Skirt and the Feather Coat, mentioned by the poet Bo Quyi (AD772–846) in his 'Song of Unending Regret':

High up where Li palace reaches into the blue,
Immortal music drifted with the wind, now here, now there;
Lazy songs, interminable dances, to the music of lyres and flutes
Till the day's end, and the Emperor tired not of gazing
Came war drums of Yu Yang, making the earth quake;
Terror silenced 'The song of the rainbow skirt and the coat of feathers'.

Chinese, Tang dynasty
late 7th century

Pair of court ladies
Earthenware with red and black pigments over white slip; height of each 36.5 cm

Gift of Sydney Cooper 1962

Photo: WERNER FORMAN

Whilst most Tang pottery tomb figures reflect secular concerns, the spiritual is cared for by images such as the magnificent and fearsome pair of unglazed guardian figures that form the centre-piece to the Tang figure displays. Such militaristic, semi-mythical figures were placed in two corners of the actual tomb chamber and, with a pair of less ferocious civilian images placed in the other two corners, were charged with the task of warding off any evil spirits that might infect the tomb. These particular figures, clearly from the tomb of an important Tang dignitary or member of the royal family, are outstanding in their detail, their sculptural quality and in the sheer vigour of their presence.

Apart from tomb figures, the Tang dynasty is distinguished by the wealth, quality and vision of all its arts. In ceramics the search for a pure white body saw the production of fine quality white wares that are the real precursors to porcelain, while the repertoire of shapes was greatly extended through contacts with the West; an initiative that is illustrated in the fine Tang glazed amphora whose shape is ultimately derived from Hellenistic prototypes.

The end of the Tang dynasty was signalled by the rebellion led by General An Lu-Shan (703–757) against the Tang emperor in AD755. His rebellion was indicative of a widespread dissatisfaction with the extravagant luxury of the court and while it was suppressed, it marked a watershed in the history of the Tang which continued to be disturbed by internal uprisings, as well as external invasions. In AD907 the non-Chinese Liao dynasty (907–1125) established itself in north China while disturbances continued in central and south China until there was once again unification with the advent of the Song dynasty (960–1279). In AD1126 the Jin, another non-Chinese people who had conquered the Liao, swept into China, forcing the Song court to flee from its capital of Kaifeng to Hangzhou in the south.

The Northern Song period (960–1126) was an era of prosperity and expansion. Kaifeng the capital flourished; the civil service developed to a high point through education and competitive examination; and there arose a new urban culture. It was a period of classical renaissance when art, philosophy and literature flourished. There were practical and technical developments too: the growth in the use of currency, the invention of movable type, gunpowder and the magnetic compass. Great progress was made in ceramics, and the wares of the northern kilns, specifically the classic wares of Ding, Yaozhou and Jun, were superior in invention and quality to those produced in southern kilns.

Examples of the classic wares of the Northern Song, so long admired by the scholars and literati of China and listed in the famous Ge Gu Yao Lun of 1388 (an early Ming publication of Chinese connoisseurship and the oldest comprehensive account of Chinese antiquities), are represented in the Gallery collections. Ding ware, the first of the classic wares to receive the patronage of the Song court, is distinguished by its thin white body, its warm, ivory coloured glaze and the fluent beauty of its carved and incised decoration. The majority of typical Ding ware bowls and dishes are

Chinese, Tang dynasty (618–906)
Horse and rider
Earthenware with *sancai* glaze;
height 40.6 cm
Gift of the Art Gallery Society 1979

bound with a protective copper rim as they were fired upside down leaving the rim unglazed. The kilns, located in Hebei province, fulfilled orders for the Song court as well as the increasingly wealthy mercantile class in the flourishing capital of Kaifeng.

Another type of special quality ware, produced at kilns located north of Xian in Shaanxi province, are the greenwares known as Yaozhou after the Song name for the area. Yaozhou ware is the most highly regarded of the various green-glazed stonewares that in the West have been grouped together as 'northern celadon'. Characteristic of Yaozhou ware is its clear, deeply incised, usually floral-inspired, decoration and its olive-green glaze colour which was praised by poets as 'mysterious' (*mi*). The Gallery's rare Yaozhou censer, in shape and decoration echoing ancient bronze prototypes, has an archaistic flavour that accords with the taste of the scholar gentleman class who used incense to create an ambience conducive to the learned pursuits of philosophy, poetry and calligraphy.

Related to the northern celadons and with a similar grey stone-ware body are the Jun wares which were produced close to the capital of Kaifeng. Their distinctive features are simple and formal shapes and the rich lavender-blue glaze derived from an iron oxide in the glaze and reduction firing (when the amount of oxygen in the kiln is reduced). These qualities are well illustrated in the Gallery's examples. Later in the Song dynasty and more particularly in the Yuan period, copper was added to the glaze to produce contrast-ing splashes of red.

The most varied, in shape and decorative techniques, of the northern kiln wares were those of Cizhou, a diverse group of stonewares produced at a very large number of kilns distributed over the provinces of Henan and Hebei. Predominantly a mono-chrome ware glazed white, black or brown, the types of decor-ation (represented in the Gallery's examples) include engraving or incising through a slip; the so-called cut-away design when the slip

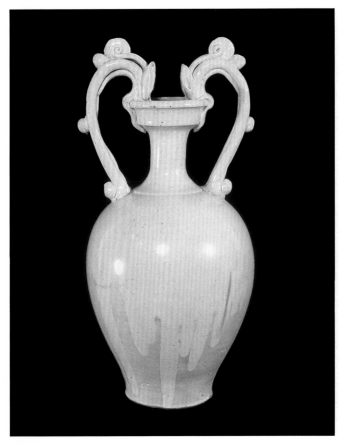

Chinese, Tang dynasty (618–906),
Amphora
Stoneware partly covered with
transparent glaze; height 30.7 cm
Purchased 1988

Chinese, Northern Song dynasty
11th–12th century
Censer on three feet
Yaozhou ware; 9 X 11.7 cm
Gift of Laurence G. Harrison 1990

is cut away to leave the design in the positive on the bare body; and painting over a slip. The potteries employed fine draughtsmen and in addition to slip decoration they occasionally decorated with low-fired coloured glazes of which the Gallery has a charming and unusual example of a swaddled baby.

After the court was forced to flee south to establish the Southern Song dynasty with its new capital at Hangzhou, it sought to recapture the cultural brilliance of the Northern Song, and the arts, particularly painting and ceramics, flourished.

Amongst the southern kilns that were imposed upon to increase and improve production under this new patronage were those of Jian in Fujian province and Jizhou in Jiangxi province. These two centres were almost exclusively concerned with the production of tea bowls. The popularity of their bowls was a response to the rise of the tea cult and an aesthetic preference for drinking pale tea out of dark glazed bowls. Such Jizhou ware glaze transmutations as 'partridge feather' and 'tortoise shell' were admired by the literati and Chan Buddhist monks. A Jizhou innovation was the use of cut-out paper patterns for reserve designs, an example of which is on show.

Hangzhou, renowned today for its scenic beauty of lakes and rolling mountains, became a grander and more resplendent city than Kaifeng. The wealth of some of its merchants was derived from the export of ceramics which were sent east to Korea and

Japan and south to Indonesia, as well as to Africa and Europe. Of the wares which enjoyed local patronage as well as being enormously popular with overseas markets, the ceramics of Longquan in Zhejiang province stand supreme. The celadons of Longquan succeeded the earlier green-glazed, high-fired Yue wares of the Tang dynasty which were admired technically for their hardness and aesthetically for their shapes and colouring, qualities without precedent in China or elsewhere. The term 'celadon', now applied to a whole range of green-glazed wares, was introduced by a French collector in the 19th century and is derived from the name Céladon, the shepherd in Honoré D'Urfé's pastoral romance *l'Astrée*, who wore ribbons of the soft grey-green colour of the Chinese ceramic wares. While a variety of decorative devices were employed on Longquan ceramics, ultimately it was admired for its colour which ranged from a pale blue-green to grey-green to olive. Song Longquan is the most esteemed as it attained an excellence of glaze and style which was never surpassed. The subtle colours and elusive beauty of celadon have been compared by poets to jade which from deep antiquity was considered the most precious of stones and symbolised the moral virtues of the Confucian scholar.

Chinese, Song dynasty (960–1279)
Teabowl with slip design of prunus blossom
Jizhou ware; 5 × 11.1 cm
Gift of Graham E. Fraser 1988

The glorious Song dynasty ended when the Mongols, who had conquered the Jin to the north in 1234, swept south to conquer China in 1279. Their period of foreign rule was to last until the restoration of Chinese rule with the Ming dynasty in 1368.

Chinese, Song dynasty (960–1279)
Teabowl with resist design
Jizhou ware; 5.5 × 10.3 cm
Gift of Graham E. Fraser 1988

Chinese, Song dynasty
12th century
Funerary vase and cover
Longquan ware; height 21 cm
Purchased 1979

CHINESE PORCELAIN

The Chinese have two basic terms for ceramics: *tao* meaning pottery in general, but also earthenware or low-fired ware; and *ci*, meaning high-fired ware whether porcelain or stoneware. The origin of the word 'porcelain' is the Portuguese *porcellana*, a cowrie shell, and its use derives from the resemblance of the shell to the translucent white body of the Chinese ceramics imported by Europe in the 16th century. Porcelain is a white, hard-paste, translucent ware made by combining kaolin, a white-firing, aplastic clay, with petuntse, a white, highly feldspathic material, and firing them to a high temperature. Europe did not discover the secret of making porcelain until the 18th century, and hence imported huge quantities of this greatly admired material.

It seems that porcelain was first made in the south of China in Jiangxi province. As early as the Shang dynasty (c1600–1027BC)

Chinese, Ming dynasty
Yongle period (1403–24)

Large dish with design of flowers of the four seasons
Porcelain decorated in underglaze blue; diam. 38 cm

Purchased 1988

Chinese, Ming dynasty
Hongzhi period (1488–1505)

Dish decorated with hibiscus spray
Porcelain decorated in underglaze
blue and overglaze yellow;
diam. 26.7 cm

Ed and Goldie Sternberg Purchase
Fund 1989

Chinese potters were making stoneware, that is, hard pottery impervious to water and fired at about 1200°C; but it was not until the Tang dynasty that porcelain was discovered after a persistent search at various kilns for a pure white, hard ceramic body. By the beginning of the 11th century the kilns in Jiangxi province, blessed with an abundance of the required materials, were producing an extremely refined porcelain with a transparent glaze of a slightly bluish cast. The name *qingbai* or *yingqing* was given to this ware which soon became an important export item, traded by the Chinese in exchange for spices, ivories and other luxury goods. When the Mongols gained control of China and established the Yuan dynasty (1279–1368), their encouragement of this lucrative trade transformed the kilns of Jiangxi, particularly those at Jingdezhen, into a series of industrial complexes. The Gallery has a few examples of *qingbai*, the most interesting of which is the small incense burner for which the prototype is the bronze *boshanlu* type believed to be a representation of Penglai-shan, the mythical abode of the Daoist Immortals.

A combination of peasant rebellions and natural disasters brought to an end the Yuan dynasty and saw the restitution of

Chinese rule under the Ming dynasty (1368–1644). Once again the arts flourished under a munificent, if introverted, imperial patronage. The tone was set by the Yongle emperor (1403–1424) who was responsible for one of the most splendid periods in Chinese history. He established the imperial capital at Beijing and was responsible for the planning and initiation of the Forbidden City which still stands today as a monument to grandeur and human aspirations. His patronage of the arts embraced a strong support of the porcelain factories at Jingdezhen which began producing porcelains of the highest quality to imperial orders.

Chinese, Ming dynasty
Wanli period (1573–1619)
Wall vase of double gourd shape
with flat back
Porcelain decorated in underglaze
blue; 32 × 15.2 cm
Purchased 1988

The use of the cobalt blue, seen on the Gallery's Yongle period dish, was relatively new at that time. Chinese potters had begun using it for decoration in the Yuan dynasty when the technique was introduced through contacts with the Near East and stimulated by the demand for showy, decorative pieces in that market. The Near East was also the catalyst for the new shapes and designs that had begun appearing in 14th century porcelain, which were inspired by Persian metal prototypes as clearly evidenced in the foliate and moulded cavetto of the Gallery's dish. The large size of such dishes was also a response to Islamic demands which forced the potters to devise methods of making a porcelain that was denser and harder, to resist the kiln hazards of firing large pieces and the possibility of damage en route to the Near Eastern markets. The demanding patronage of Yongle and his court achieved new standards in every department of the manufacture of porcelain: the paste was finer in grain and of a pure whiteness, the potting more skilful, the forms more elegant, and the decoration more refined. The centre of the Gallery's dish is decorated with the favourite theme of the Flowers of the Four Seasons.

Other fine Gallery examples of 15th century porcelain decorated in underglaze blue include a stemcup of the Xuande period (1426–1435), and a deep bowl dating to circa 1455. The stemcup was for use in Buddhist rituals when it was filled with clear water and placed on an altar. Its decoration is appropriately Buddhist: the Eight Buddhist Emblems of the wheel of the law, the conch shell, the canopy, the vase, the paired fishes, the umbrella, the lotus and the endless knot, each surmounting a lotus bloom, the Buddhist symbol of purity. Both the stemcup and the bowl bear the characteristic technical feature of an unevenness in the blue colour. Termed 'heaped and piled', this effect, in fact a lack of control of the blue, is esteemed by connoisseurs, and later 18th century potters sought to emulate it, usually without success.

The Gallery has two fine dishes from the short-lived Hongzhi period (1488–1505). One is decorated in underglaze blue with the rare design of a single dragon among lotus and water weed; the

Chinese, Ming dynasty
Wanli period (1573–1619)
Dish with design of dragon and two phoenixes
Porcelain decorated in *wucai* enamels; 4 × 26.9 cm
Purchased 1988

other is decorated in underglaze blue and overglaze yellow, with a finely painted design of a hibiscus spray. Decorations such as these were designed by the most regarded artists at the imperial court in Beijing and the drawings sent to the porcelain factories to be copied. The blue and yellow dish is one of the great classics of Ming porcelain. While the pattern was created in the Xuande period, the use of the yellow ground became the most popular treatment for this design and perpetuated the tradition of the 'imperial' yellow reserved for the use of the emperor. From early Chinese texts on ceramics we know that pieces of the Hongzhi period were most admired, both for the perfection of the body and for the quality of the yellow glaze. Chinese connoisseurs were particularly sensitive to the quality of the tone of yellow which was praised if it was the soft colour of steamed chestnuts or the brightness of sunflowers. The yellow on the Gallery's dish is particularly good. The draughtsmanship of the design is exemplary: the central hibiscus spray elegantly fills the space in complete harmony with the form of the dish, while the sparsely distributed leaves and branches are beautifully placed in relation to each other.

By the beginning of the 16th century the Ming dynasty had passed its zenith and was entering a gradual decline. The porcelain has a different quality to the refined perfection of 15th century porcelain: bodies are more robust. decoration more exuberant and often more colourful. Illustrated books provided new sources of inspiration for designs which became more informal and naturalistic in order to achieve a wider appeal. The main technical innovation was the introduction of medium-fired lead silicate glazes used in a variety of techniques. In one the design is executed in coloured glazes in conjunction with incised outlines, for example, the green and yellow stemcup of the Zhengde period (1505–1521), and in another the design, for example dragons, was painted with wax resist so that after the piece had been glazed and fired, the design was left in the fired body (biscuit) against a glazed ground. The biscuit design was subsequently filled in with a coloured enamel, usually green, and refired. Such pieces are striking in their impact, particularly the green and yellow wares which are called Ming *sancai* (three-colour). An important innovation of the later Wanli period (1573–1619) was to apply more than two colours onto the biscuit. The Gallery has a charming example of this important technique that was the forerunner of the later *famille verte* enamels on biscuit.

The Jiajing (1522–1566), Longqing (1567–1572) and Wanli (1573–1619) periods stylistically may be considered together. While there was a decline in quality, partly due to the enormous orders from the palace which allowed the potters less time for care, pieces of merit and spirit were produced. Examples are the Jiajing dish decorated in a rich blue with the motif of the Three Friends (prunus, pine and bamboo; symbols of purity, strength and integrity), and the Wanli wall vase with a popular figurative subject of scholars in a garden. Successful also during this period was the use of the colourful *wucai* (five colours) enamels when underglaze blue was combined with overglaze enamels. A lively Daoist-inspired example of *wucai* decoration is the Gallery's Wanli period dish with a central yellow dragon beneath the motif of three horizontal lines that signifies heaven and is the first of the Eight Trigrams. The dragon, flanked by two phoenixes, rises above a rock and wave pattern suggestive of the Eastern Seas of the Daoist paradise.

The drop in imperial orders for porcelain that accompanied the decline of the Ming was compensated for by overseas orders, particularly from the Dutch and the Japanese. The period from about 1620 to 1680 that coincided with stormy political upheavals is called the Transitional period and was a time of change in styles and techniques, prompted by foreign demands and the absence of court-imposed stereotypes. A particular type of blue and white that made its debut in the late 16th century and in all probability was made exclusively for export was the ware known as *Kraak-porselein* after the Dutch name for the Portuguese *carracks*, or merchant ships, which carried the wares to Europe. Another type of ware catering to Japanese taste was *ko-sometsuke* ('old blue and white') which is distinguished by its casual decoration, eccentric shapes and defective edges where the glaze has broken away (an effect prized by the Japanese who term it *mushikui*, 'insect eaten'). These export wares, together with later ones of the Qing dynasty, are displayed together in a separate section of the Gallery.

When the Manchus overran China to establish the Qing ('Pure') dynasty, although they were non-Chinese (in fact it was their ancestors who ruled north China during the Jin dynasty 1115–1234), they had little influence on China's cultural life. During the Qing dynasty (1644–1912) most porcelain was produced at Jingdezhen, and can be classed into three types: *guanyao*, imperial or official ware, *minyao* or popular ware, and export ware. Imperial ware was produced at workshops set up and supervised by controllers appointed from the imperial household. The finest porcelain of the period was made between 1680 and 1753 after the emperor Kangxi (1662–1722) instigated a regeneration of the Jingdezhen kilns by appointing talented director Zang Yingxuan (1680–1688) who was then succeeded by two more exceptional men — Nian Xiyao (1726–1735) and Tang Ying (1736–1753).

The number, colour and design of porcelain used at the court was strictly regulated and manufactured only at the imperial kilns.

Chinese, Qing dynasty
Kangxi period (1662–1722)

Bowl with design of two dragons pursuing two flaming pearls
Porcelain decorated in underglaze blue; 7.8 × 16 cm

Gift of J. Hepburn Myrtle in loving memory of the late Miss V. (Pussy) Abernethy 1987

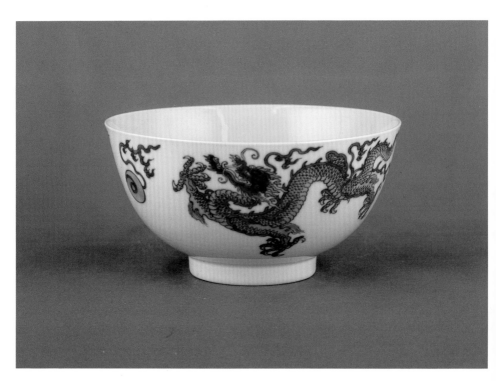

Chinese, Qing dynasty
Kangxi period (1662–1722)

Pair of vases, each decorated with a
bird perched on a prunus branch
Porcelain with *famille verte*
decoration; heights 28.5 and 27.5 cm

Purchased 1965

These wares were made for household and ceremonial use as well as for imperial gifts. All official wares were exclusively for use within the court whilst the demand from those outside the court for similar high quality pieces was satisfied by private kilns at Jingdezhen.

The porcelain of the Kangxi period has a pure white body, smooth, clear glazes and skilfully applied, vibrant decoration. Examples of Kangxi blue and white are the bowl decorated with the design of dragons pursuing a flaming pearl, and the ginger jar decorated with prunus blossom on a cracked ice background, a pattern much in vogue in the Kangxi period. Such jars were used for gifts presented on the occasion of the Chinese lunar New Year that falls in late January or February coincidental with the end of winter when the prunus first buds.

Apart from blue and white, the main porcelain production of the Kangxi period was *famille verte*, a term coined in the middle of the 19th century by the French ceramic collector, Albert Jacquemart, to refer to the prevailing colour in the overglaze decoration. This type, together with the related *famille noire* and *famille jaune*, evolved from the Ming polychrome traditions. Towards the end of Kangxi *famille rose*, a pink derived from gold chloride, was introduced.

Chinese, Qing dynasty
Yongzheng period (1723–35)
Dish with design of five red bats
flying around a fruiting peach tree
Porcelain with *doucai* decoration;
diam. 15.5 cm

Purchased 1965

The Gallery has a varied collection of Kangxi *famille verte*, of which the finest pieces are the two vases on attached simulated wood bases. Both vases have the same design but executed by different hands. This particular design would seem to indicate the dependence of ceramic decorators on woodblock printed manuals, for it is almost an exact replica of a work by the famous bird-and-flower painter Chen Hongshou (1598–1652) who contributed to such manuals, and who was an innovative exponent of the academic style of bird-and-flower painting that had gained prestige in the Southern Song dynasty. Illustrated books were probably also the source of the design on the large *famille verte* vase on show, while Daoism provided the imagery of Xi Wangmu, Queen Mother of the West, and the spotted deer, a symbol of longevity, which appear on a large dish. The peach that so gracefully decorates another dish is inscribed with the gold seal characters *wan shou*, 'a myriad longevities', the imperial birthday greetings.

Birthday greetings and Daoism are implied in a classic dish of the Yongzheng period (1723–1735) which is decorated with a scene of five red bats (*wu fu*, a homonym for the Five Happinesses which are health, wealth, many sons, a long life and a peaceful death), peaches (symbols of longevity), and waves (indicating the Daoist Eastern Seas in which are located the Isles of Immortality). This small dish of exquisite quality is also of interest technically. In line with the Yongzheng and Qianlong (1736–1795) periods' keenness to revive classic Ming techniques and glazes, the dish is decorated in the *doucai* ('contrasting colours') technique of underglaze blue outlines filled in with overglaze enamel colours, a technique first perfected in the Chenghua period (1465–1487), at the height of Ming innovation.

Throughout the Kangxi, Yongzheng and Qianlong periods, monochromes were an important and beautifully varied class of wares. The largest group is that of the copper reds which range from the deep to the palest and are produced by firing in a reducing atmosphere. On show is a red *meiping*, a purely Chinese shape specifically designed for the display of a branch of flowering plum. Blue, turquoise and green monochromes are included in this group.

The Qianlong reign is regarded as the most impressive period of Qing history. The emperor was a devotee of the arts and an enthusiastic collector of porcelains, even having his own poems inscribed on pieces as seen on the overglaze iron-red teabowl on display. The official wares of Qianlong are technically faultless, confident in style and decoration and determinedly Chinese in all respects with a clear preference for long-established and archaistic patterns and shapes. Characteristic of such styles is the Gallery's moonflask where the shape has a Ming prototype, and the dragon is painted in underglaze copper red which, for reasons of expense

Chinese, Qing dynasty
Qianlong period (1736–95)

Moonflask with a design on each side of a dragon and a flaming pearl
Porcelain decorated in underglaze blue and underglaze red;
height 30.5 cm

Purchased 1964

Chinese, Qing dynasty
late 17th century
Figure of Guanyin
Blanc de chine; height 34.4 cm
Gift of Sydney Cooper 1962

and the difficulty of manufacture (the red pigment is difficult to fire because of its volatility), is often restricted to official wares.

From the Qianlong period on, a separate type of monochrome ware was produced for ritual use by the emperor. These vessels, a sample of which is displayed separately, were catalogued in a book called *The Illustrated Regulations for the Ceremonial Paraphernalia of the Qing Dynasty* compiled in 1759. The pieces were made in forms derived from ancient bronzes and their colour was determined by which Beijing temple they were made for, such as yellow for use in the Temple of Earth and blue for the Temple of Heaven. A related category of wares comprised those made for the Buddhist altars in the palaces and temples of Beijing and Chengde, the Qing court's summer retreat. Characteristic of this type of ware is the Gallery's altar vase where the decoration is Buddhist and the shape probably derived from a pewter Lamaist prototype.

The 19th century saw disastrous economic and political problems in China, but production of imperial porcelain was maintained until 1911, with little reduction in the levels of either quantity or quality of technical accomplishment.

Although it is the production of Jingdezhen that has been considered, there were other porcelain production centres. The centre whose products matched the quality of Jingdezhen was Dehua in Fujian where the porcelain, known in the West as *blanc de chine*, was made for local and overseas markets. The Gallery has some fine and unusual pieces, such as the moulded figures of Guanyin, and an exquisitely modelled and richly glazed brushrest. A large family of provincial porcelains, often with vigorously painted decoration, are those identified as Swatow and exported in large quantities to Europe and other parts of Asia.

CHINESE PAINTING

In China calligraphy is revered above all other arts. Calligraphy reflects the moral calibre and spirit of a person; and ever since it first appeared in the form of angular pictographs scratched into oracle bones of the Shang dynasty (c1600–1027BC), it has been the foundation of the unity and uniqueness of Chinese culture. Calligraphy appears in various styles from the formal to the cursive, from ancient bronze inscriptions to the modern simplified *pinyin* system. It also appears everywhere and is so consummately integral to Chinese artistic expression that wherever it appears, whether on a painting, a ceramic, a bronze or even bamboo, the calligraphy assumes a natural role in the complete expression. Its contribution in the fine and applied arts is not only literary, ideological and philosophical, but also aesthetic.

From as early as the 8th century, calligraphy was linked with painting and poetry to form the 'Three Perfections'. Prior to that, in the late 5th century, the great critic Xiehe had articulated the 'six principles' of painting which remained relevant to all subsequent painting. The first and most important of these principles was 'spirit resonance' (*qi*) according to which the task of the artist was to attune himself with the cosmic spirit that vitalises all things.

The greatest tradition throughout the history of Chinese painting has been the literati or *wenrenhua* tradition. This tradition, formulated in the 11th century by a group of scholars led by the philosopher, poet and painter Su Dongpo (1036–1101), held that the arts were a branch of philosophy, and that a painting should reflect the quality not of the subject, but of the man. The ideals of this tradition were expressed by the 'Four Great Masters' of the Yuan dynasty (1279–1368) who epitomised the sage-scholar-painter. These men refused to co-operate with the foreign Mongol government and retreated into a private world where they gained inspiration from nature, from the arts of the past, and from the fellowship of their scholar-gentry friends. Since their priority was the expression of personal character and scholarship, they scorned professional styles and virtuosity of brushwork, but prized amateurishness and technical awkwardness (*zhou*) while also filling their paintings with stylistic and literary references to the great masters of the past. Landscape painting was the primary vehicle for their self-expression, but certain plants, specifically the 'Four Gentlemen' (orchid, bamboo, chrysanthemum and plum) were also popular because they were easy to paint, and imbued with symbolism.

The superiority of the *wenrenhua* tradition was fully articulated in the late Ming dynasty by the painter and theorist Dong Qichang (1555–1636) who formulated the distinction between the scholarly, amateur artists and court/professional artists by applying the terms 'southern school' and 'northern school' to the two traditions. This division was based on an analogy with two schools of Buddhism: the southern school which held that enlightenment was a sudden, spontaneous achievement, and the northern school which maintained it was a gradual, progressive achievement. His theories became particularly relevant in the Qing dynasty when once again scholars chose to withdraw from public life rather than collaborate with the Manchus. There were two groups of his followers: the Orthodox school which received court patronage, and the so-called 'Individualist' painters who carried on his creative approach to painting, and were inspired by the more revolutionary aspects of his style. These artists, particularly Zhu Da (1626–1705) and Dao Ji (1641–1707) were to have enormous influence on 20th century

Group of scholar's items:

(LEFT) Brushrest, Kangxi period (1662–1722)

Blanc de chine, 5.4 × 10.5 cm;

Purchased 1987

(MIDDLE) Brushpot, late 18th/mid 19th century

Porcelain simulating carved bamboo, 12.7 × 6.8 cm;

Gift of Laurence G. Harrison 1977

(RIGHT) Brush washer, Kangxi period (1662–1722)

Celadon, 7.3 × 7.9 cm;

Purchased 1988

artists through their spirited, spontaneously brushed paintings that were free of all kinds of restraints.

Because of the respect accorded painting and calligraphy, all the items needed by a scholar are carefully selected and assessed in terms of their individuality, rarity, antiquity, and even tactile quality. Scholars were collectors and connoisseurs of porcelains, jades, bronzes and ivories, as well as paintings. On the scholar's desk were to be found the 'Four Treasures' of paper, brush, inkstone and inkstick, as well as all the other accessories necessary for writing and painting: a water dropper, brushpot, wrist rest, brush washer, and seals (seal carving was a highly regarded skill).

The Gallery has some fine examples of scholars' items amongst which is a beautifully conceived *blanc-de-chine* brushrest, modelled in the form of a dragon resting on the shores of the Isles of Blest on which grew the *lingzhi* fungus of immortality. Grotesque and contorted forms such as the rocks in this piece were sought out as objects for the scholar's desk for they were at once fascinating to handle and contemplate, while being regarded as containing the quintessence of spiritual forces, *qi*, which is all the more active when held in distorted shapes.

Brushpots come in all sizes and all media. Amongst those in the collection, one has the particularly apt decoration of Li Bo (701–762), China's most famous poet, reading. This pot is also of interest as it is made of porcelain but simulates bamboo. Chinese artists took great delight in simulating one material in another and transgressing the borders between materials.

The majority of the Gallery's collection of Chinese paintings are modern. Modern Chinese painting has its roots in the 19th century in Shanghai. After China's defeat in the Opium War of 1842, Shanghai became one of the five treaty ports open to foreign trade. Its merchants became wealthy and sought decorative painting, unfettered by the literary and antiquarian allusions that inspired traditional literati paintings. A popular artist who catered to the new, restless spirit in Shanghai was Ren Bonian (1840–1896), whose style was indebted to popular folk art for an infusion of vigour and fresh subjects. The Gallery's painting by Ren Bonian is typically a lyrical and naturalistic depiction of a figure scaled large in relation to its environment. With the advent of the Shanghai school, figures and birds-and-flowers supplanted the long-established pre-eminence of landscape as a subject for painting.

A major Shanghai artist who studied under Ren Bonian was Wu Changshuo (1844–1927). Wu was a member of the scholar-gentry class and passed the civil service examination in 1865, but decided against pursuing the career of an official, preferring to devote all his energy to art. He began practising seal-carving and calligraphy

REN BONIAN, Chinese, 1840–1896

Figure standing in a boat 1893
Hanging scroll; ink and light colour on
paper, 114.3 × 48.2 cm

Purchased 1988

Inkstone with inscriptions by Wang Zhen and Wu Changshuo;

33.3 × 20.3 cm

Purchased 1989

WU CHANGSHUO, Chinese
1844–1927

Loquats 1919
Hanging scroll; ink and colours on paper, 181.5 × 82 cm

Purchased 1987

before painting, but became prominent in all spheres. His seal-carving style traced its ancestry to the style of the Han dynasty, while in calligraphy he was highly regarded for his expertise in many styles, ancient and contemporary.

For his painting subjects, Wu concentrated on flowers or boughs with blossom or fruit, as illustrated in the Gallery's painting of loquats. The painting was executed in 1919 when Wu was seventy-five, and a consummate master of the brush, evident from the rich layering of ink and the verve and energy contained in the composition. The calligraphy is exemplary, with a movement, rhythm and dynamism that can only be achieved through continuous practice and discipline. The long inscription reveals Wu's affinity with past traditions where the content and style of the calligraphy was a critical feature of both the composition and the harmony of a painting. Wu profoundly influenced many younger artists such as Pan Tianshou (1897–1971) who became one of China's most highly regarded bird-and-flower painters. Pan was distinguished for his bizarre, cranky, often amusing images of birds, realised in rich, black ink, and strong brushwork emanating a crude energy.

Wang Zhen (1867–1938), a wealthy Shanghai businessman, was a student of both Ren Bonian and Wu Changshuo. Wang, a devout Buddhist, started painting quite late in his life, but became famous for his Buddhist figures and his calligraphy. The Gallery's painting by Wang is an intense portrait of Bodhidharma, the Indian prince who brought the doctrine of Chan (or Zen) Buddhism to China in the early 6th century, and is revered as the First Patriarch. The title of the painting is *Nine years facing the wall* (*Mian bi jiu nian*), a phrase central to Zen teaching. The phrase refers to a famous legend concerning Bodhidharma's nine years of implacable 'wall gazing' at the Shaolin temple. In Chan texts, 'wall gazing' was a metaphor for the inexplicable suddenness of enlightenment, but in paintings the interpretation is often quite literal. The first line of calligraphy on the right of the painting, which can be freely translated as 'The heart determines one's appearance', was written by Cai Yuanpei (1868–1940), the leading liberal educator of China during the early years of the Republic who, as Minister of Education in 1912, advocated aesthetic education as one of the five tenets of an ideal education system.

The Gallery has, amongst its scholars' items, an exceptionally large inkstone which Wang Zhen inscribed in 1921 with a self-portrait of himself as a monk and a poem which states that in his previous life he was a monk. Wu Changshuo has also inscribed this inkstone in his typically energetic and exemplary calligraphy.

The giant of the modern movement of Chinese painting was Qi Baishi (1863–1957), the most illustrious 20th century Chinese

PAN TIANSHOU, Chinese
1897–1971
Bird and bamboo
Hanging scroll; ink and colour on
paper, 46.5 × 58 cm
Purchased 1985

painter, with a far-reaching influence. Born into a poor farming family in Hunan province, he was apprenticed to a carpenter while painting at night. At twenty-seven he began formal painting studies, adopting first the *gongbi* ('fine brush') style (to be seen in his treatment of the dragonfly in the Gallery's painting), but then concentrating on the expressive *xieyi* (literally 'delineate idea') style of painting which stressed the spontaneous, summarily-executed approach. Qi's particular metier was bird-and-flower painting, and his paintings brim with vitality and freshness, while demonstrating his unmatched talent for reducing things to their absolute essence. Qi studied nature meticulously and relished painting the everyday, whether it was birds and flowers that were free of traditional literary associations, or even vegetables. Qi loved to paint vegetables — pumpkins, turnips, bamboo shoots — and took great pride in his 'smelling of vegetables', that is, his rustic simplicity. In his use of colours, he skilfully drew upon the vivid colours of Chinese folk art. In his later years he was recognised by the

QI BAISHI, Chinese, 1863–1957

Gourds on trellis
Hanging scroll; ink and colours on
paper, 137 × 61 cm
Purchased 1986

People's Republic of China as a truly great, honest and original artist. Amongst the awards bestowed on him was the honour of 'People's Artist', by the Chinese Ministry of Culture in 1953.

Qi's influence has extended well into the present day and many of the Gallery's paintings represent artists working in a similar *xieyi* style. A major Shanghai artist represented in the collection is Lu Yanshao (born 1909). Lu's distinctive representation of the landscape, characterised by sloping, jagged mountains, raging torrents and swirling clouds, was developed in the 1930s in Sichuan province where he was forced to go because of the Sino-Japanese war. His idiosyncratic, dynamic style is marked by his brilliant exploitation of negative space and the flashes of red colour which accentuate the black of his inks.

While artists such as Wu and Qi evolved their personal style in the late 19th/early 20th century and maintained it, artists who were born later were affected by the turbulent times in which they lived. The political upheavals and policy changes that have scarred China throughout the 20th century have been mirrored in changing art styles: the first decade of this century saw the influence of contemporary Western and Japanese art; the early years of the Republic (1912-1949) saw the promotion of a realism based on the French academic style; the 1930s were notable for the graphic woodcut movement that later incorporated Mao Zedong's view, expressed in his famous 'Talks on Art in the Yenan Forum' of 1942, that art must serve the workers; and the 1950s were marked by strong Soviet Social Realist influence.

In 1905 the imperial court of the Qing dynasty abolished the civil examination system, and subsequently a system of public schools was established with art courses, including ones on Western art, introduced into the curriculum. In the first half of the 20th century the challenge of Western art was taken up by many artists, but never with the same impact wrought on Japanese art in the 19th century. Some Chinese artists travelled overseas to study, to Europe or Japan.

Outstanding among those who studied in Europe was Xu Beihong (1895-1953) who studied in Europe for eight years before returning to an unsettled China in 1927. Xu's hallmark is the spirited galloping horse typified in the Gallery's example. In such horse paintings can be seen the result of his studies of Western concepts of perspective foreshortening, anatomy and the expression of mass and volume. Xu's great contribution was to enrich traditional Chinese painting with Western ideas and concepts but without prejudice to traditional Chinese techniques or aesthetics.

One traditional practice of Chinese art that persisted into the 20th century was for an artist to specialise in one genre, and just

XU BEIHONG, Chinese, 1895–1953

Galloping horse 1944
Hanging scroll; ink on paper, 61 ×
49.5 cm

Purchased 1988

as Xu focused on horses, so Wu Zuoren (born 1908), a pupil of Xu's who also studied in France, concentrated on camels and pandas. Both he and Xu indirectly in their work reflect the impact of the devastating Sino-Japanese War of 1935–45, for both had to abandon the oil painting they had adopted after their overseas training because the conflict stopped the importation of oil pigments. The war drove millions of people westwards and Wu's monochrome ink depictions of the yaks and camels of the Chinese steppes were his response to this forced change in environment.

Among the artists who studied in Japan was Fu Baoshi (1904–1965), a self-taught scholar, who absorbed the lessons of his own traditions as well as studying Western and Japanese art to develop a strong, personal style. Another versatile traditional artist was Zhang Dajian (1899–1983), whose wartime stay in Dunhuang in the far northwest from 1941 to 1943 affected his subsequent art which was much affected by Tang and Song dynasty painting styles that he had seen in Buddhist wall paintings at the Dunhuang cave temples.

During the 'Black Decade' of 1966 to 1976 that embraced the Cultural Revolution and the influence of Jiang Qing, Mao's wife and leader of the so-called Gang of Four, traditional artists were attacked and severely persecuted. As a result artists either did not work or submerged their individuality in anonymous, politically acceptable group projects.

Since then, painting has begun to flourish again, showing a blending of the traditional and the modern with a new originality and artistic freedom, leading to a wide spectrum of styles and themes. Many of the most talented artists work in the xieyi style, but the Gallery also has paintings in the descriptive meticulously rendered gongbi style. This particular style, for centuries scorned by the literati, has a long history of neglect, but it is perhaps indicative of the experimentation and lack of artistic prejudice that it is now one of many styles being re-evaluated and given new interpretations.

JAPANESE PAINTING

The majority of the Gallery's collection of Japanese painting dates from the Edo period (1615–1868) to the present day. The Edo, or Tokugawa, period witnessed an era of unprecedented peace and prosperity in Japan after centuries of civil strife between warring feudal lords (*daimyō*). When the *daimyō* family of Tokugawa gained power, Tokugawa Ieyasu took the title of Shogun, perpetuating a 400 year tradition unique to Japan where the emperor, residing in his court at Kyoto, was the titular head of the nation, but real political power was vested in the Shogun.

The Tokugawa government (*bakufu*) adopted various measures to ensure they maintained their power. A new capital was established at a village called Edo (now Tokyo and still the capital of Japan) and all *daimyō* were compelled to spend several months of

DETAIL
Views in and around Kyoto c1660
Pair of six-fold screens; ink, colour and gold on paper, each screen 136.5 × 383.5 cm
Purchased with funds donated by Kenneth Myer 1980

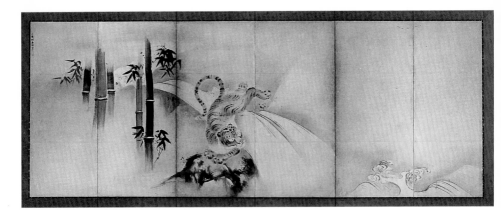

KANŌ TAN'YŪ, Japanese,
1602–1674
Dragon and tiger c1640s
Pair of six-fold screens; ink on paper,
each screen 133.5 × 351.5 cm
Purchased with funds donated by
Kenneth Myer 1989

each year there and to leave their families in residence when they returned to their fief. Fear of foreign aggression prompted the adoption of an isolationist policy whereby no Japanese was allowed to leave the country, and foreign contact was restricted to a few Chinese and Dutch traders at the one port of Nagasaki. Culturally this encouraged the refinement of indigenous styles while restrictions on travel within Japan helped nurture regional variations.

To ensure the continuing political and cultural dominance of the samurai class, a strict social hierarchy of samurai, farmer, craftsmen and merchant, was instigated, and the *bakufu* issued regulations on the code of behaviour expected of samurai. This code demanded excellence in the warrior-traditions of martial arts, archery and horsemanship, as well as in the civilian arts of painting, calligraphy, poetry, *nō* theatre, tea ceremony (*chanoyu*), and Chinese and Japanese literature and history. In aspiring to cultural pre-eminence, the samurai drew heavily on the classical aristocratic traditions which had been so superbly articulated at the imperial court of the Heian period (794–1185) before ruling power shifted from the court aristocracy (*kuge*) to the samurai (*bushi*); and on the Chinese cultural traditions, in particular those of Zen Buddhism, adopted by the first Shoguns in the 12th century. These two traditions — the sumptuous, colourful and decorative native one, and the minimal, suggestive and sober imported one — are responsible for the duality of the traditional Japanese aesthetic.

While the *daimyō* of the Edo period were the inheritors and perpetuators of these classical traditions, there arose new traditions under the patronage of a merchant class that grew rich on profits made as a result of general prosperity and the shift from an agricultural economy where rice was the medium of exchange

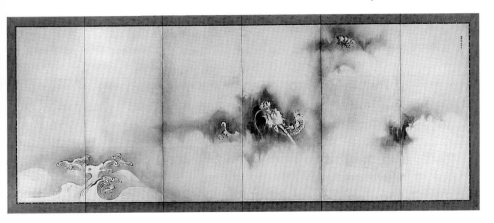

to a money economy. The most outstanding new school catering to the taste of the townsmen (chōnin) was ukiyo-e.

Edo art was overwhelmingly secular in nature, partly because of the bakufu's suppression of Buddhist establishments which had been major patrons of art in the past. On the other hand, one outcome of the bakufu's insistence on the samurai study and adoption of Confucianism, designed to inculcate the proper notions of loyalty, honour and reverence for one's superior amongst the samurai, was the new nanga school of landscape painting based on Chinese prototypes.

Examples of the traditional arts patronized by the daimyō in the Edo period are on show in the first section of the Japan Gallery. The pair of landscape screens by Unkoku Tōeki (1591–1644) who traced his artistic lineage back to Sesshū (1420–1506), the greatest master of suibokuga (ink painting), is an atmospheric rendition of an ideal landscape through which the viewer can transcend the mundane.

Apart from landscape, animals symbolic of power and the forces of nature were popular subjects with the daimyō patrons. Such is the case with the screens by Kanō Tan'yū (1602–1674) of a dragon and tiger, for in China the dragon is identified with yang, the male principle representing spring, rain, sun and light; and the tiger with yin, the female principle representing autumn, wind, the moon and darkness. To a Japanese samurai, the tiger also served as a symbol of strength and virility. Kanō Tan'yū was the patriarch of the Edo branch of the Kano family, for centuries painters to the Shogun and the official practitioners of the Chinese derived suibokuga tradition in Japan. Tan'yū, as chief painter to the bakufu was a much respected and influential painter. This pair of screens

Japanese, Genroku period
(1688–1703)

Mount Sumiyoshi
Single six-fold screen; ink and colours
on gold ground paper
150.5 × 288 cm

Purchased 1987

DETAIL
KUSUMI MORIKAGE,
Japanese, c. 1620–1690

Rural landscape with horses and cows
Pair of six-fold screens;
ink and gold wash on paper,
each screen 151.5 × 349 cm

Purchased with funds donated
by Kenneth Myer 1984

can be dated to the 1640s based on their stylistic affinities with two other important tiger and dragon commissions he received: the sliding door paintings (*fusuma-e*) in the Abbot's residence of the Kyoto monastery of Daitoku-ji (1641), and the ceiling painting in the famous Tōshōgū shrine at Nikko.

A significant artist who began his career in Tan'yū's studio but was then expelled for his intransigence was Kusumi Morikage (c1620–1690). The Gallery's pair of screens by Morikage, considered to have been painted while he was still in Tan'yū's studio, is a fluently brushed landscape in which specific passages, such as the horses cavorting with their young in the contagious ebullience of a spring day, heighten the overall mood of rural tranquillity. Already in this work, Morikage's nascent interest in the everyday activities of farmers can be detected and in his later rural scenes he was to prove himself a pioneer in the development of genre painting.

DETAIL
Japanese, Rimpa school, 17th century

Flowers of the four seasons
Pair of six-fold screens; ink, colour and sprinkled gold on coloured paper, each screen 153 × 348 cm

Purchased with the assistance of The Sidney Myer Fund 1989

Genre incident had appeared in earlier paintings, but usually as incidental embellishments to the main court or religious narrative. It was only with the growth of the cities that paintings of manners and customs (*fusokuga*) developed as a separate category of painting. At first they were commissioned by the court and samurai: such is the case with the popular *Rakuchū-rakugai zu* screens presenting panoramic views of Kyoto in the 16th and 17th centuries. The Gallery has a fine example of this genre which through the accurate rendering of buildings can be dated to around 1660. The

view is one looking to the east across the Kamo River towards the Higashiyama hills. The lower section of each screen below the Kamo River is *rakuchū* ('within the city'); above the river is *rakugai* ('without the city'). The dominant building on the right screen is the Great Buddha Hall; while the most significant buildings on the left screen which depict Kyoto north of Shijō (Fourth Avenue) are the imperial residences. The screens are crowded with fascinating vignettes of daily life: archery competitions, theatre performances, and the normal business of the blacksmiths, scroll mounters, lacquerers and drapers in their shops lining the busy streets. In the use of bright, high-keyed colours, the linearity of figures and buildings, and the generally detailed miniature style the screens reveal their debt to the indigenous *yamato-e* tradition of painting.

Another important early genre screen in the collection is a single one depicting Mount Sumiyoshi, close to the old port of Sakai in Osaka. According to legend, the Sumiyoshi Shrine that appears on the hill on the left, was founded by Empress Jingō (reigned 201–269). This Shinto shrine, believed to offer protection and prosperity for mariners and fishermen, is balanced in the composition with the depiction of fishermen on the lower right. From extant examples we know that this screen, depicting spring and summer activities, would originally have been paired with a left-hand screen depicting autumn and winter on Matsushima (literally 'Island of Pines'), glorified in literature and poetry as one of the three most beautiful scenic spots in Japan.

A new school of art that arose in Kyoto in the early Edo period was Rimpa. Drawing much of its inspiration from the classical painting and literature produced at the court during the Heian period (794–1185), this school was responsible for a brilliant revival of traditional aristocratic arts — not only painting, but also ceramics, lacquer and textiles.

Representative of this style is a sumptuous pair of screens bearing the seal 'Inen' which is found on paintings from the workshop of Nonomura Sōtatsu (?–1643?), one of the founders of Rimpa. The screens' subject of Flowers of the Four Seasons is a popular one in Japan where there has always been, in literature, poetry and painting, a great sensitivity to the changing of the seasons. The different flowers, each with its own symbolic or poetic associations, are skilfully placed across the surface and beautifully realized in the rich colours typical of Rimpa.

A more subtle and restrained example of Rimpa is the two-fold screen bearing the seal of Watanabe Shikō (1683–1755). Using only silver for the moon, gold for the clouds and mists, and ink, the artist evokes the deep quietude of an uninhabited place at night. Less typical of Rimpa paintings is the portrait by Sakai Hōitsu

SAKAI HŌITSU, Japanese
1761–1828
Portrait of Abbot Zetsugai c1803
Hanging scroll; ink and colours on silk, 102.1 × 51.2 cm
Purchased 1983

61

(1761–1828) of Abbot Zetsugai who, until his death in 1713, was the 241st abbot of the Kyoto temple Myōshin-ji. Such portraits, termed *chinzō*, have a long history in Zen Buddhism where they were customarily presented to a disciple on the successful completion of his studies with a master. This is the only known such portrait by Hōitsu who was responsible for revitalizing Rimpa in the early 19th century and for bringing it to Edo from Kyoto.

The culture created by the newly-affluent class of townsmen (*chōnin*) in the Edo period was so distinctive and pervasive that the word *ukiyō* was adopted to describe it. *Ukiyō* was a term originally used in Buddhist texts to refer to the transient, ultimately sadly irrelevant nature of the pleasures enjoyed in this life. The *ukiyo* culture, in Edo centred on the licensed entertainment district of Yoshiwara, affected literature, music, theatre and art. The art of the floating world (*ukiyo-e*) had two principal subjects: the courtesans of the pleasure quarters, and Kabuki actors. A small early *ukiyo-e* screen in the Gallery's collection graphically portrays the interior of one of the pleasure quarters.

The depiction of courtesans was a special category of painting termed *bijin-ga*, literally 'paintings of beautiful women'. In *bijin-ga* an individual's personality was conveyed not through individual facial expression but by pose, gesture and the choice and colour of her kimono. *Bijin-ga* were symbols of a feminine ideal. The Gallery has several fine examples of *bijin-ga*, of which the earliest is Miyagawa Chōshun's portrayal of an *onnagata*, a female impersonator of the Kabuki theatre.

Exceptionally large and beautiful is a painting of a high-class courtesan (*yūjo*) by Utagawa Toyoharu (1735–1814), founder of the Utagawa school that dominated *ukiyo-e* through the 19th century. From the distinctive hairdo of the sumptuously-robed courtesan the painting can be dated to the 1780s when such hairstyles, with their wide side flanges and abundance of combs and ornamental hairpins, were the vogue.

A more poignant note is struck by Shun'ei's painting where the poem above, written by a noted poet of the day, conveys the misery of a courtesan's life: from the inscription we gather that the courtesan, who is twenty-seven, laments the ten years she has spent in the bitter sea (a metaphor for becoming a prostitute), regarding it now, as she is about to leave, as a mirage (the word 'mirage', *shinki*, has the same pronunciation as 'hardship').

This same poet, Ota Nampo, has also inscribed, along with six others, a painting in the collection by Kubo Shumman (1757–1820). The poems, all written in the cursive style of *gyōsho* (running script) are witty and topical, full of references to the Yoshiwara and its courtesans. The painting is a good example of the type of joint

KUBO SHUMMAN, Japanese
1757–1820
Courtesan standing beneath a tree
c1800
Hanging scroll; ink and slight colour on silk, 94.2 × 31.6 cm
Purchased 1980

MIYAGAWA CHŌSHUN, Japanese
1683–1753

Portrait of an *onnagata* of the Kabuki
theatre
Hanging scroll; colours on paper
110 × 53 cm

Purchased by the Art Gallery of
New South Wales Foundation 1987

work popular with Edo artists and poets who often formed clubs so they could meet together and combine in producing such paintings in a spirit of entertainment. Another example in the collection is a painting of the Six Immortal Poets, each one painted by a different pupil of Hokusai.

Poetry also appears in the paintings of the *nanga* or *bunjinga* school that was strong through 18th and 19th centuries. This style followed Chinese prototypes of the Ming dynasty and was popular with amateur as well as professional artists throughout Japan. Most of the Gallery's examples of *nanga* are by artists of the third generation. Among these, the outstanding example of the poetic heights *nanga* could attain is the painting by Matsumura Goshun (1752–1811) in which a fisherman, the *nanga* archetype of the ideal secluded life, wends his way through a sylvan setting which has

UTAGAWA TOYOHARU
Japanese, 1735–1814
Portrait of a standing courtesan
1780s
Hanging scroll; ink and colours on silk, 161.5 × 84.2 cm
Purchased with funds donated by Kenneth Myer 1990

DETAIL
HOKUSAI PUPILS
The Six Immortal Poets c1830
Hanging scroll; ink and colour on weathered paper, 94 × 28.5 cm
Purchased 1983

MATSUMURA GOSHUN
Japanese, 1752–1811

Fisherman returning home c1785
Hanging scroll; 110 × 33 cm

Purchased under the terms of the
Florence Turner Blake Bequest 1984

DETAIL
MATSUMURA GOSHUN

Fisherman returning home c1785

TANI BUNCHŌ, Japanese
1763–1840
Mountains in the early summer rain
1826
Hanging scroll; ink on paper
174 × 96 cm
Purchased with funds donated by
Kenneth Myer 1987

been rendered with the most delicate and seductive ink and colours. Goshun was also a *haiku* poet as were the artists Ki Baitei (1734–1810) and Yokoi Kinkoku (1761–1832), whose works are also represented in the collection.

After his *nanga* phase, Goshun was influenced by the work of Maruyama Ōkyo (1733–1795), founder of the Maruyama school and an important Kyoto artist whose style is represented in the collection with a pair of screens depicting cranes. Ōkyo is credited with revitalizing late Edo painting by emphasizing the accurate sketching from nature and by injecting his work with a realism derived in part from his studies of Western pictorial devices. His naturalistic renderings of birds, animals and flowers met with widespread success and he had many pupils. An outstanding but eccentric artist who was expelled from Ōkyo's conservative studio was Nagasawa Rosetsu (1754–1799) who became esteemed as one of the great Individualist painters of Japan. Portraits of Zen eccentrics, such as in the Gallery's painting of Kanzan and Jittoku, were a popular choice of subject for Rosetsu who also fulfilled commissions from Zen temples.

Goshun drew on the lyricism of *nanga* and the naturalism of the Maruyama school to found the Shijō school. The charming and unpretentious style of this school is illustrated in the works of Kono Bairei (1844–1895), Suzuki Nanrei (1775–1844) and Kishi Chikudō (1826–1897).

A towering figure in late Edo artistic circles was Tani Bunchō (1763–1840), a painter to the *daimyō* Matsudaira Sadanobu and for many years an influential advisor to the *bakufu*. Bunchō's eclecticism and stylistic diversity can be credited perhaps to his research in publishing in 1800 an eighty-five volume set on the Chinese and Japanese art held in Japanese collections. While he is regarded as a *nanga* artist and was responsible for its spread to Edo, he was also responsible for the definition of *nanga* being much wider in Edo than Kyoto. Hence an artist such as his pupil Tsubaki Chinzan (1801–1854) was grouped with *nanga*, although his delicate flower paintings for which he preferred the 'boneless' technique where colour creates its own outlines without being confined by ink contours, have also been influenced by Chinese Qing dynasty bird-and-flower painting which was popular in the late Edo period.

To date most of the Gallery's collection of later pictorial material of the Meiji (1868–1912) and subsequent periods is in the form of prints and albums and hence is not on show in the Japan Gallery but will be shown on occasion in the Gallery's Prints and Drawings Gallery on Level 2.

JAPANESE ART

Two main types of neolithic culture have been distinguished in Japan: the earlier one known as Jōmon ('rope pattern') after the impressed pattern which decorates its pottery; and the later, dating roughly from 200BC to AD250, known as Yayoi after the area in Tokyo where its characteristic pottery was first found. Yayoi pottery is the true ancestor of the Japanese ceramic tradition and is represented in the Gallery by a large impressive jar made for special events such as harvest festivals.

The Japanese regard for ceramics outstrips that of any other nation. The connoisseurship of ceramics can be largely credited to the tea ceremony (*chanoyu*). Initially, during the 12th century, tea drinking in the style of boiling water poured over powdered green tea (*matcha*) in an open bowl, was practised by Zen monks as a stimulant during their long sessions of meditation. However it was soon adopted as a social custom by both the aristocracy and *daimyō*. At first the finest imported Chinese objects were used in lavish, formal ceremonies, but then there evolved a unique aesthetic that found beauty in the simple, the unobtrusive, and the humble. From this aesthetic developed a distinct style of tea ceremony called *wabi*, or 'poverty', tea which was a quest for spiritual fulfilment in the ideal of poverty. The ideals of *wabi* tea were most fully articulated by Sen no Rikyu (1552–1591), esteemed as the greatest tea master (*chajin*) of all time. After him, the tea masters who practised *wabi* tea became the arbiters of taste in Japan, formulating a unique style of tea ceremony through which the celebrant sought to excite in his guests an aesthetic experience comparable in the West to the spiritual experience engendered by religious rituals.

The influence of the tea ceremony on the culture and arts of Japan has been so pervasive that a traditional tearoom has been incorporated into the Gallery's displays. This fully working tearoom (*chashitsu*) includes a space in the centre for the kettle used to boil the water for tea, a small area to prepare and clean the utensils, and a large alcove for the display of works of art (*tokonoma*). The design and materials of this tearoom encapsulate those qualities esteemed in Japanese aesthetics: simplicity, irregularity and impermanence. Simplicity is found in the natural materials of wood, bamboo and stone; irregularity is found in the asymmetrically juxtapositioning of the odd and the contradictory, while impermanence

70

Japanese, Yayoi period
(200BC–AD250)
Ceremonial jar
Earthenware; height 34 cm
Purchased with funds donated by
Kenneth Myer 1986

is found in the use of natural materials and living flowers. The emotive appeal of the ephemeral was articulated by the 12th century poet Kenkō when he perceptively wrote: 'If man were never to fade away like the dews of Adashino . . . but lingered on forever in the world, how things would lose their power to move us. The most precious thing in life is its uncertainty'.

The aesthetics of *chanoyu* elevated the most utilitarian pieces into aesthetic objects. For example, the Gallery has two large Shigaraki storage jars which in their scale and honesty of purpose exemplify Japanese pottery of the Middle Ages. When large jars like these first appeared in response to economic changes in farming methods in Japan, they were strictly utilitarian pieces produced for the use of their local communities as seed or fresh-water

71

Japanese, Muromachi period
(1392–1568)
Large jar
Shigaraki ware; height 53 cm
Gift of Norman Sparnon 1988

storage jars. Shigaraki wares, easily recognisable by their characteristic, quartz-flecked clay, invariably have an uneven shape because
they were formed by the ancient technique of coiling and smooth-
ing. However it was this very simplicity and unpretentiousness that
endeared them to the teamasters who praised them for seeming
hiekareta, 'chilled and withered', and incorporated them into the
repertoire of tea utensils.

The two most important tea utensils are the tea caddy (*chaire*)
and the tea bowl (*chawan*), examples of which are included in the
displays. Most native ware tea ceramics are of pottery which the
Japanese aesthetic preferred over porcelain. Bodies and glazes are
subdued, in line with the understated aesthetic called *shibui*, and
every piece is individually shaped with no use of mass production
techniques such as moulds. Tea bowls are modest sculptural state-
ments in clay.

NAKAZATO TARŌEMON
Japanese, born 1923

Large jar
Tataki (paddled) Karatsu ware;
height 33.6 cm

Gift of the Rev. Muneharu Kurozumi
1981

Traditional potteries represented in the collection are Bizen, Seto, Shino and Satsuma. Admired amongst teawares are Karatsu wares, first made by emigré Korean potters who came to Japan in the wake of Japan's unsuccessful incursion into Korea in the late 16th century. A Karatsu *mizusashi* (fresh-water jar for the tea ceremony) in the collections is a classic example. The persistence of many of these traditions into modern times is seen in the Gallery's excellent collection of contemporary ceramics. A vigorously modelled jar by Nakazato Tarōemon (born 1923), a Living National Treasure since 1951, symbolizes the vitality of ceramic traditions. Nakazato carefully studied the techniques of old Karatsu ware to produce jars such as the Gallery's *tataki* (paddle-beaten) piece where the stamped decoration and paddled form have their ultimate source in Korean Punch'ong ware. The tradition of Bizen, esteemed as one of the 'Six Old Kilns' of medieval Japan, is well represented in the Gallery's modern collection with pieces by masters such as Fujiwara Kei (1899–1983) and Kaneshige Tōyō (1896–1967), both designated Living National Treasures for their work in revitalising the Bizen tradition.

The teamasters found great beauty in some of the everyday tea and rice bowls of southern China and Korea. Twelfth century Jian and Jizhou wares with their subtly variegated *temmoku* glazes were

KANESHIGE TŌYŌ
Japanese, 1896–1967

Tea bowl inscribed 'Every day is a new day'
Bizen ware; 7.8 × 12–12.6 cm

Gift of the Rev. Muneharu Kurozumi 1986

Japanese, Edo period, late 17th
century

Dish decorated with tiger and
dragon
Kakiemon porcelain; diam. 18.3 cm
Purchased 1983

brought back from southern China by visiting Zen monks while
imported coarse and unsophisticated rice bowls of ordinary Korean
peasants profoundly influenced the taste of tea masters. An unre-
strained admiration for fine Chinese porcelain, lacquers, and paintings was maintained by *daimyō* culture and resulted in a rich blending of Chinese and Japanese artefacts in the tea ceremony. Chinese
porcelain types popular with teamasters were the 16th century
kinrande porcelains with their gilt over red designs, and vigorously
painted eccentric blue and white porcelains. Tea utensils were
assessed not only in aesthetic terms, but also in terms of their
antiquity and personal associations. Exceptional pieces became her-
editary treasures and some were even conferred with their own
name. Because of the admiration accorded such Chinese wares
examples of them are included in the Japanese displays.

Porcelain was first made in Japan in the early years of the 17th
century, some eight centuries later than its first manufacture in
China. The four main types of porcelain are Imari, Kakiemon,
Kutani and Nabeshima. With the exception of Nabeshima which
was made by one *daimyō* for his own household use and as pres-
entation pieces, the porcelains were produced for local and overseas consumption. While pottery always maintained a superior

status in Japanese connoisseurship, porcelains were popular within Japan, particularly the 'brocaded' wares of Imari.

The Gallery owns several pieces of Imari including an interesting blue and white map plate made for local use, as well as large and impressive plates and jars made for export. Japanese porcelains became extremely popular in Europe when the Dutch East India Company began to import them as substitutes for Chinese porcelains after the political and economic turmoil that accompanied the fall of the Ming dynasty interfered with Chinese porcelain production. Imari wares were the most commonly exported, whether blue and white plates decorated in the Chinese *Kraak* style, or brocade wares. Amongst the Gallery's Imari wares is a large covered jar for the export market, unusual in being decorated only in red and gilt. In the 19th century the brocade style was maintained by the Satsuma kilns which produced pieces for the local and foreign markets. Fine examples in the Gallery of pieces made for Japanese consumption include a large jar dated to 1805, and a small piece persuasively modelled as a bamboo cricket cage wrapped in a richly decorated *furoshiki*, that marvellously practical cloth invention in which the Japanese can carry anything.

Amongst the Gallery's examples of Kakiemon porcelain is a vigorously painted plate that epitomizes the style. Characteristically for Kakiemon, the design is Chinese (in this case a tiger and dragon) executed in vibrant enamel colours, while the body is a warm, rich white against which the motifs are delicately and sparsely placed. Typical too of Kakiemon is the rust-red coating on the rim. On viewing such pieces, one can understand the passion for Kakiemon that developed in Europe where it was first copied by Meissen and later in England by the Chelsea, Bow and Worcester factories.

The Gallery's square Kutani vase is distinguished by the vigour of its designs interspersed with a classic Kutani diaper pattern. The firing cracks in this piece have been obviously repaired with gold lacquer. Unlike the Chinese whose inclination is to discard faulty pieces, the Japanese exploit such faults, revelling in them as symbols of the uncertainty of fate and man's inability to control the element of fire even within a kiln.

Although the Japanese adopted the use of lacquer from the Chinese, they perfected it into an artistic tour-de-force of superb craftsmanship and imaginative design. Japanese call their lacquer, made from the sap of the lacquer tree (*Rhus vernicifera*), *urushi,* and the most popular way of decorating it was called *maki-e* (literally 'sprinkled picture'), which was achieved by sprinkling gold powder onto the lacquer surface.

Noted contemporary writer Tanizaki Jun'ichirō (1886–1965) captured the appeal of lacquer when he wrote in his essay 'In

Japanese, Edo period, 17th century
Suzuribako (writing box)
Lacquer; 4.2 × 22 × 23.1 cm
Gift of Klaus Naumann 1989

Praise of Shadows': 'Lacquerware decorated in gold is not some-
thing to be seen in a brilliant light, to be taken in at a single glance;
it should be left in the dark, a part here and a part there picked
up by a faint light. Its florid patterns recede into the darkness,
conjuring in their stead an inexpressible aura of depth and mystery,
of overtones but partly suggested. The sheen of the lacquer, set
out in the night, reflects the wavering candlelight, announcing the
draughts that find their way from time to time into the quiet room,
luring one into a state of reverie'.

Throughout Japanese history fine lacquer was a symbol of
status, prosperity and artistic sensibility. One class of objects on
which imaginative designs were realised with consummate skill was
the writing case (*suzuribako*), the most honoured lacquer object of
secular use and the essential possession of every person of education. Because of the high regard accorded writing, the instruments of writing have always been treasured in both China and
Japan, but the creation of a box especially designed to accommo-
date the necessary inkstone, inksticks, brushes and water dropper,
seems to have been a Japanese invention, already in evidence by
the Heian period (794–1185). The Gallery's *suzuribako*, as well as
its rectangular box decorated with poppies against a black background, attest the virtuosity of the lacquer artist.

Lacquer was used for the boxes in which elaborate sets of
games were stored. One such game was the incense game, the
object of which was to distinguish different kinds of aromatic woods
by their scent when they were burnt. Such connoisseurship of
incense was an accomplishment of the Kyoto aristocracy from the
10th century and it was subsequently refined into an elaborate
social activity on a par with *chanoyu*, although it never became as
widespread because it was a more rarified and expensive pastime.

MINAGAWA KIEN
Japanese, 1734–1807
Wrist rest inscribed 'Who knows the
mind of Heaven and Earth?'
Bamboo, 19.4 × 5.3 cm
Purchased with funds donated by
Mr L. Phillips 1980

The different instruments needed in the game were stored in beautifully decorated *kōdansu* (incense boxes) of which the Gallery's example is of exquisite craftsmanship.

In the displays the emphasis is on those pieces most admired by the Japanese themselves. However, with the social and political reorganisation of the early Meiji period (1868–1912) when the class of highly skilled craftsmen (*shokunin*) ceased to exist, and Japan embarked on a process of Western industrialisation, there developed a huge export trade in objects catering to Victorian taste. New ceramic factories sprang up to produce, amongst other things, the large pieces favoured in Victorian interiors; and the many highly skilled artisans who had once catered to the intense demands of the samurai for arms and armour, turned their talents to decorative bronzes. To display the qualities of such wares, the Japanese Government encouraged participation in the Great International Exhibitions that distinguished the late 19th century. Japan exhibited in Vienna in 1873, in Paris in 1878, and in Sydney in 1879. The Gallery possesses many of the pieces exhibited in Sydney, a gift of the Japanese Government on completion of the exhibition.

Japanese, Edo period, 17th century
Covered box decorated with poppies
Maki-e lacquer;
13.5 × 22.7 × 14.6 cm
Purchased 1988

The 19th century French movement of bronze animal sculptors, the Animaliers, had a profound effect on certain Japanese metal craftsmen resulting in bronze tigers, eagles and human figures. The Gallery has an unusual representation of a bronze kangaroo that belongs to this tradition.

The inherent vigour, life and sensitivity for the material that is so characteristic of Japanese artistic traditions continued to flourish into the 20th century. Today the innovative and distinctive creative instincts of Japanese artists and craftsmen are stimulated not only by their own traditions, but also by Western styles and visions and by the possibilities of technology. And yet whilst always absorbing and adapting, the Japanese artists of today maintain an aesthetic that will always be Japanese.

DETAIL
Japanese, 19th century
Kōdansu (box for the incense game)

Japanese, 19th century

Kōdansu (box for the incense game)
Lacquer; 12.6 (with stand 17.8) ×
17.7 × 11.7 cm

Purchased 1988

SUZUKI OSAMU, Japanese
born 1926

Square vase on pedestal foot
Stoneware; height 19.5–23 cm;
diam 13 cm

Gift of Norman Sparnon 1988

SOUTH-EAST ASIAN ART

The South-east Asian collections embrace the art of Cambodia, Thailand, Vietnam and Indonesia. Apart from Vietnam in whose culture the Chinese influence predominated, these civilizations were indebted to India as the source of inspiration that shaped their religions, literature, philosophy and art. From India came both Buddhism and Hinduism. There are two major traditions of Buddhism: the Mahayana tradition which is found in China, Korea, Japan and Vietnam, and the Hinayana or Theravada tradition found in Burma, Cambodia and Thailand. Hinayana Buddhism holds that salvation is an individual concern and that there is little one person can do for another; central to Mahayana Buddhism is the concept of the bodhisattva, a being who has reached the point of achieving

Thai, 14th century
Sawankhalok ware Jar
Celadon; 14 × 19 cm
Purchased 1967

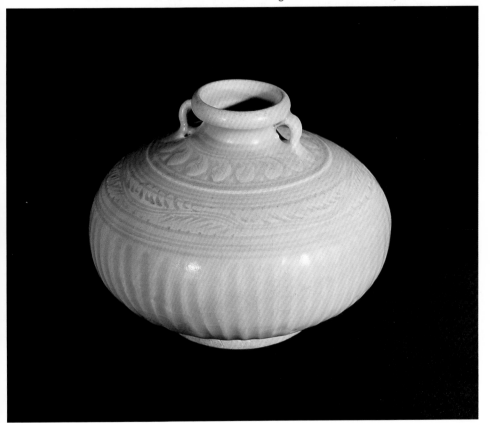

Nirvana, or Buddhahood, but who postpones his own enlighten-ment until others have achieved the same level. Bodhisattvas do not appear in Hinayana Buddhism in which one of the most com-mon images is the seated Buddha with his right hand 'touching the earth' in the religious gesture (or *mudrā*) referred to as 'Buddha subduing Mara' which is symbolic of the Buddha's power over evil. Legend has it that just before enlightenment, the historical Buddha Gautama was meditating beneath a tree when he was approached by Mara, the God of Desire and Death, intent on preventing him attaining enlightenment. Mara coaxed and threatened the Buddha who finally extended his right hand to touch the earth and summon up the Earth Goddess who rose with her long hair streaming with water. By wringing out her hair she swept away Mara, leaving the Buddha victorious. This image of the Buddha appears in stone and bronze throughout Southeast Asia.

From the time of the earliest missionaries around the 5th cen-tury AD, Buddhism has permeated the entire population of Thailand and provided a unity of thought and artistic activity that persists today. The inspiration for painting and sculpture has been, for centuries, predominantly Buddhism. Much of the painting is in the form of temple murals but movable sculpture is more access-ible. All Buddhist statuary is governed by strict and well-defined canons of Buddhist iconography and no liberties or personal whims on the part of a sculptor can be tolerated. Ancient texts outlined the thirty-two characteristics of Buddha which sculptors aimed to capture, for example, hands like lotus flowers just beginning to bloom, a nose like a parrot's beak, eyebrows like drawn bows, and hair like the stings of scorpions.

Evidence of Thai culture before the introduction of Buddhism is provided by the bronze and clay artefacts excavated at the village of Ban Chiang in northeast Thailand in 1966. Scientific tests on these finds dated the objects as far back as 3000BC, thus prov-ing that Thailand had a culture predating that of Mesopotamia, until then regarded as the cradle of civilization. Examples of Ban Chiang ceramics from the earliest unglazed black wares to the later pieces with red ochre painted decoration are in the collection.

The Dvaravati kingdom lasted until the 11th century when it was conquered by the westward expansion of the Khmer empire. The Khmer kingdom had begun its transformation into an empire in the 9th century under the reign of Jayavarman 11 (802–850), and from the 10th to the 12th centuries the Angkor kings enjoyed a Golden Age during which they built huge cities and temple com-plexes, symbolic of their power and divinity.

The Gallery's Khmer collection can only hint at the past glories of this magnificent civilization. The major piece is the standing stone

Khmer c1000AD
from Koh Ker
Guardian lion
Sandstone; height 84 cm

Purchased 1987 with funds donated by Ross H. Adair, Tim and Prue Allen, Bruce R. Bockman, Madeleine Boulken, Joanna Capon, Graham M. Cole, S. M. Gazal, Bruce C. Hudson, Rodney T. Hudspeth, Daryl Isles, J. G. Jagelman, N. Jeffreson, Michael Magnus, D. A. M. McCathie, Rosalind O'Connor, Lesley Pockley, G. & E. Sternberg, Freddy Storch, Robert Whyte and Ken Youdale

lion which would have once been a conspicuous feature of one of the awesome Hindu temple complexes built by the Angkor kings. Such lions were placed on terraces and stairways to guard the central pyramidal structure that symbolised Mount Meru, the residence of the gods at the centre of the Hindu world. Lions were not native to Cambodia and the Khmer sculptors devised their own fanciful interpretations of these royal guardian figures. The characteristic full, frontal pose and upright stance lend the figure a composed regal air, while in the elaborately carved demonic head and patterned chest can be seen the Javanese influence so important to the development of Khmer culture.

The 10th century Hindu culture of Central Java is exemplified in the Gallery's collection by the stone sculpture of Ganesha, the elephant-headed Hindu god of good fortune and success, who has always been popular in Java. Images of Ganesha were usually found near those of Siva and his consort Parvati in a temple. However in Java they are also found alone near rivers and ravines to protect travellers. The most distinctive feature of Javanese representations of Ganesha is his pose. The manner of sitting with the soles of his feet touching is unknown in India but is found in Java and Cambodia. Originally his four arms would have held his attributes: a broken tusk, a fly whisk, a rosary and a cup of sweets.

The influence of the Khmer tradition on Thai sculpture is to be seen in pieces of the Lopburi school that was active in central and northeastern Thailand between the 10th and 14th centuries. Lopburi sculpture is generally divided into two periods: the first, or Angkorian, period (10th–12th centuries) when the Thai sculptors produced an officially recognised Khmer style; and the second, or late, Lopburi period when the local Thai artisans evolved a modified style of their own in the 13th and 14th centuries as the dominance of the Khmer influence began to wane. The Gallery has a sculpture belonging to this second, more significant period. The figure is most likely a Buddhist deity since Buddhism had supplanted Hinduism within the Khmer empire by the late 12th century. The Khmer influence is seen in the emphasis on volume in the modelling, and in the clothing, for the short *dhoti* with its fish-tail pleat and the wide belt decorated with incised rosette motifs are characteristically Khmer.

Khmer ceramics offer a unique facet of the Asian ceramic tradition and reflect an indigenous culture free of other influences. Unlike other Southeast Asian ceramics, the Khmer products were made solely for the local populace and not for export. Fundamentally a peasant pottery, the wares were not patronised by the wealthy Khmer, and had completely disappeared by the 14th century due to the fierce competition offered by the technically

Central Javanese, 10th century

Figure of Ganesha
Volcanic stone; 67 × 40 cm

Anonymous gift 1985

Thai, 13th century
Lopburi style
Figure of a deified male
stone; height 94 cm
Purchased with the assistance of
funds provided by S. M. Gazal, Mrs
M. Gowing, Bruce C. Hudson, Mr &
Mrs D. Isles, J. G. Jagelman, Mr &
Mrs A. Morris, Mrs Kerry Packer,
G. & E. Sternberg, Freddy Storch

superior, imported Chinese celadons and porcelains. However many of the pieces have a sculptural presence and serenity comparable to that found in Khmer sculpture. Examples in the Gallery's collection include a large elephant-shaped jar which exemplifies the popularity of zoomorphic vessels in the Khmer repertoire; a rare anthropomorphous covered jar which was used as a funerary vessel; and a more typical vase of baluster form with a wide flanged mouth. All pieces are covered in the technically flawed but characteristic smooth, brown glaze. The vase would have been a temple fitting, used for holding lotus blossoms in Buddhist ceremonies, while the elephant shaped jar could be an exceptionally large example of the diverse class of lime pots, used to contain the lime paste which was smeared on a leaf of the *piper betle* before a mix containing shavings of the hard areca nut was added. (The abundance of lime pots attests to the popular addiction to betel leaf chewing which played an important social role through the vast area stretching from India to the Pacific.)

After the decline of the Khmer empire, a federation of neighbouring kingdoms in central Thailand was formed to create the kingdom of Sukothai, the first Thai nation. Simultaneously the north was united into the Lanna kingdom with its capital at Chiang Mai. The Sukothai period was relatively short-lived (13th–15th centuries), but its second king Ramkamhaeng is one of the great figures of Thai history, credited with many innovations including the adoption of the Khmer alphabet into the Thai language. The bronze sculptures of Sukhothai are considered the apogee of Thai artistic endeavour and the Gallery has a classic Sukhothai Buddha head that typifies this style. Thai bronzes were made by the 'lost wax' method in which a wax mixture was applied to a modelled clay core, then etched with the desired features, and covered with a thick layer of clay. The entire piece was then baked in a kiln and, after the wax had melted and run out, the clay mould was cooled before being filled with molten bronze which occupied the areas vacated by the melted wax. When the bronze had hardened, the mould was broken away and discarded.

The Sukhothai kingdom is also distinguished by the florescence of ceramic creativity that occurred. Some wares were produced at kilns close to the city of Sukhothai, but another larger class of wares known as Sawankhalok were produced at kilns centred around the city of Si Satchanalai, north of Bangkok. Sawankhalok kilns produced an astonishingly wide variety of wares ranging from large water jars and architectural ornaments to tiles, ewers, kendis, dishes, jarlets and miniature figures. Sawankhalok wares can be divided into several categories on the basis of the decoration, the largest category being the underglaze black decorated wares, of

Khmer, 11th–12th century
Elephant-shaped jar
Stoneware, height 21 cm
Purchased 1981

which there are examples in the collection. Typical of the ware is the medium grey, black speckled body, and the compartmentalised patterns of geometric and vegetal motifs. A shape unknown in the underglaze black repertoire, but typical of Sawankhalok celadon is that of the Gallery's beautifully toned celadon jar. Another category is that of the so-called 'brown and pearl' wares, of which the Gallery has some characteristically small examples, such as a water dropper in the form of a blowfish, and an incense holder in the form of a kneeling woman.

The wares of Sawankhalok are well known since they were widely traded throughout Southeast Asia, and examples have been found in burial sites throughout the Philippines and Indonesia. The wares of the numerous kilns of the northern kingdom of Lanna, not all of which have yet been identified, are less well known. The Gallery has some fine examples of these northern kilns, for example, a tall, round jar from the Sankampaeng kilns in a district east of Chiang Mai in which is located a prosperous silk and cotton weaving town of the same name; a Paan ware dish with a simple,

Khmer, mid 12th century

Bottle with anthropomorphic
features
Stoneware; height (with lid) 26 cm

Gift of Mr F. Storch 1981

incised linear design under a celadon glaze of which the character-istic colour is the slightly yellowish-green of young rice; and a Kalong ware dish with its distinctive, bold, black and cream design. Northern wares such as these only came to public attention in 1984 when a major archaeological find at Tak near the Burmese border unearthed numerous burial sites crammed with Chinese, Vietnamese and Northern Thai ceramics.

In 1438 Sukhothai was subjugated by Ayutthaya which had been founded to the south in 1350. The Burmese conquered Lanna in 1558 and it was to remain their territory until the late 18th century. They then attacked Ayutthaya, which repelled them in the 1590s, to enjoy nearly two centuries of peace as the capital of Thailand, and to become one of the great cities of the world. However in 1767 the Burmese struck again, completely destroying Ayutthaya. The remnants of the population moved downriver to Thon Buri, and in 1782 to Bangkok which has been the capital since.

In the Bangkok period, the patronage and glorification of Buddhism continued to be the principal theme of the arts. The

Thai, 13th–14th century Jar
Sankampaeng ware; height 28 cm
Gift of Mr F. Storch 1986

Thai, 18th century
Bowl decorated with *thepanom* and
norasingh
Bencharong porcelain; 95 × 20 cm
Gift of Mr F. Storch 1985

Gallery's image of the seated gilt Buddha sheltering under the seven headed *naga* is typical of the showy glitter cherished at this time. This particular image is derived from a story concerning the historical Buddha, Gautama: in the fifth week of the seven weeks he meditated after attaining Enlightenment, the Buddha was seated at the edge of Lake Muchalinda when a terrible storm arose, causing the waters of the lake to rise. Seeing that Buddha was lost in thought, the *naga* king Muchalinda slipped his coils under Buddha's body, lifting him above the flood. At the same time, he spread the hoods of his seven heads to shelter him.

Thai taste of this period is also seen in the two categories of Chinese ceramics made and decorated to accord with it: Bencharong, or five-colour, wares, and Lam Nai Thong, or goldwashed, wares. The Gallery owns an exceptionally fine piece of 18th century Bencharong which may well date to within the Ayutthaya period (1350–1767) when this style arose. The bowl is decorated in deep and varied colours with alternating images of *thepanom* and *norasingh*, both minor Buddhist deities. Typically the *thepanom* sits crosslegged in a praying posture, nude except for a

petalled collar, bracelets and crown, while the *norasingh*, believed
to reside in the mythical Himaphan forest in the Himalayan mountains, has a human head, the hindquarters of a lion with a flame-
tipped tail, and the hoofs of a deer. Other examples of Bencharong
are typically richly decorated and ostentatious.

Thailand was governed by an absolute monarchy until 1932, and
then by a constitutional monarchy, but still today the monarchy and
Buddhism are the basis of Thailand's art and culture.

Thai, 15th century
Dish
Kalong ware; diam. 20.5 cm
Purchased 1989

Thai, Bangkok period, 19th century

Buddha enthroned under seven
headed *naga*
Gilt bronze; 64.5 × 74.5 cm

Purchased 1948

CHRONOLOGICAL TABLES

CHINA

Neolithic	c5000–c1700BC
Shang dynasty	c1700–1027BC
Zhou dynasty	1027–221BC
Qin dynasty	221–206BC
Han dynasty	206BC–AD220
Northern and	AD220–581
Southern dynasties	
Sui dynasty	581–618
Tang dynasty	618–906
Five dynasties	906–960
Song dynasty	960–1279
Yuan dynasty	1279–1368

Ming dynasty 1368 to 1644

Hongwu	1368–1398
Yongle	1403–1424
Xuande	1426–1435
Chenghua	1465–1487
Hongzhi	1488–1505
Zhengde	1506–1521
Jiajing	1522–1566
Longqing	1567–1572
Wanli	1573–1619
Tianqi	1628–1643

Qing dynasty 1644 to 1912

Shunzhi	1644–1661
Kangxi	1662–1722
Yongzheng	1723–1735
Qianlong	1736–1795
Jiaqing	1796–1820
Daoguang	1821–1850
Xianfeng	1851–1861
Tongzhi	1862–1873
Guangxu	1874–1907
Xuantong	1908–1912
Republic	1912–1949
People's Republic	1949–

JAPAN

Jōmon	to c200BC
Yayoi period	c200BC–cAD250
Kofun (Tumulus)	cAD250–552
period	
Asuka period	552–646
Nara period	646–794
Heian period	794–1185
Kamakura period	1185–1332
Nambokuchō period	1333–1392
Muromachi period	1392–1568
Momoyama period	1568–1615
Edo (Tokugawa)	1615–1868
period	
Meiji period	1868–1912
Taishō period	1912–1926
Showa period	1926–1988
Heisei period	1989–

KOREA

Three Kingdoms

Kokuryo dynasty	37BC–AD668
Paekche dynasty	18BC–AD663
Old Silla dynasty	57BC–AD668
United Silla Kingdom	AD668–936
Koryo period	918–1392
Yi dynasty	1392–1910
Japanese rule	1910–1945

Republic of Korea in the South; Democratic
Republic of Korea in the north 1948 to present.

THAILAND

Prehistoric	to AD100
Indianized (Hindu)	100–500
period	
Dvaravati (Mon)	500–1000
period	
Srivijaya period	700–1200
Lopburi period	900–1300
Sukhothai period	1200–1400
Lanna period	1200–1500
Ayutthaya period	1350–1767
Thon Buri period	1767–1782
Bangkok period	1782 to present

CAMBODIA

Neolithic period	c4000–100BC
Funan period	ADc100–400
Chenla	c400–550
Pre-Angkorian period	c500–799
Angkorian period	802–1431
Post-Angkorian	
period	1431 to present

VIETNAM

Chinese rule	111BC–AD939
Ly dynasty	1009–1225
Tran dynasty	1225–1400
Le dynasty	c1420–1787